126 SEX POSITIONS GUARANTEED TO SPICE UP YOUR BEDROOM

INCREASE YOUR SEX EDUCATION WITH SEXUAL POSITIONS FOR COUPLES

AVENTURAS DE VIAJE

Illustrated by
NEIL GERMIO

Copyright SF Nonfiction Books © 2015

www.SFNonfictionBooks.com

All Rights Reserved
No part of this document may be reproduced without written consent from the author.

WARNINGS AND DISCLAIMERS

The information in this publication is made public for reference only.

Neither the author, publisher, nor anyone else involved in the production of this publication is responsible for how the reader uses the information or the result of his/her actions.

CONTENTS

Introduction   xi

MAN ON TOP

Position 1. 1st Posture	3
Position 2. 2nd Posture	4
Position 3. 3rd Posture	5
Position 4. 4th Posture	6
Position 5. Bridal Bridge	7
Position 6. Backward Bending Flower	8
Position 7. 7th Posture	9
Position 8. 8th Posture	10
Position 9. Ape	11
Position 10. 10th Posture	12
Position 11. 11th Posture	13
Position 12. Level-Feet	14
Position 13. Pine Tree	15
Position 14. Rising Star	16
Position 15. Splitting	17
Position 16. Tail of the Ostrich	18
Position 17. Swallows In Love	19
Position 18. Yawning	20
Position 19. Dragon Turns Away	22
Position 20. G-Spot Stimulator	23
Position 21. Crab	24
Position 22. Dragon Turn	25
Position 23. Galloping Horse	26
Position 24. Gaping	27
Position 25. Gripping With Toes	28
Position 26. Huge Bird Above a Red Sea	29
Position 27. One Who Stops at Home	30
Position 28. Placid Embrace	31
Position 29. Pressing	32
Position 30. Raised Feet	33

Position 31. Refined Position	34
Position 32. Silkworm Spinning a Cocoon	35
Position 33. Stopperage	36
Position 34. Twining	37
Position 35. Clasping	38
Position 36. Fixing a Nail	39
Position 37. Half Pressed	40
Position 38. Horse Shakes Feet	41
Position 39. Splitting Of Bamboo	42
Position 40. Ankle Hold	43
Position 41. Fetal Flower	44
Position 42. Encircling	45
Position 43. Held Feet	46
Position 44. Horse Cross Feet	47
Position 45. Intact Posture	48
Position 46. Jade Joint	49
Position 47. Joining the Lotus	50
Position 48. Lotus	51
Position 49. Mandarin Duck	52
Position 50. Phoenix Playing in a Red Cave	53
Position 51. Pressed	54
Position 52. Pumping the Well	55
Position 53. Turning	56
Position 54. Rising	57
Position 55. Turtle Move	58
Position 56. Wife of Indra	59

WOMAN ON TOP

Position 57. Butterflies in Flight	63
Position 58. Fish	64
Position 59. Interchange of Coition	65
Position 60. Inverted Embrace	66
Position 61. Sharing Reins	67
Position 62. Accomplishing Position	68
Position 63. Alternative Movement of Piercing	69
Position 64. Frog Fashion	70
Position 65. Kama's Wheel	71
Position 66. Crying Out	73

Position 67. Lotus Inverted	74
Position 68. Loving Lift	75
Position 69. Paired Feet	76
Position 70. Position of Equals	77
Position 71. Singing Monkey	78
Position 72. Snake Trap	79
Position 73. Yin and Yang	80
Position 74. Ascending Position	81
Position 75. Butterfly	82
Position 76. Cat and Mouse Sharing a Hole	83
Position 77. Catbird Seat	84
Position 78. Love Seat	85
Position 79. Orgasmic Role-Reversal	86
Position 80. Pair of Tongs	87
Position 81. Race of the Member	88
Position 82. Hanging Bow	89
Position 83. Spider	90
Position 84. Goat and the Tree	91
Position 85. Mare	92
Position 86. Rabbit Grooming	93
Position 87. Reciprocal Sights of the Posteriors	94
Position 88. Reverse Crab	95
Position 89. Swing	96
Position 90. Spinning the Top	97
Position 91. Topping and Turning	99

FROM BEHIND

Position 92. 6th Posture (Doggy Style)	103
Position 93. Loving Chair	104
Position 94. Rising Pillows	105
Position 95. Standing Doggy	106
Position 96. Tiger Step	107
Position 97. White Tiger	108
Position 98. Cicada on a Bough	109
Position 99. Coitus from Behind	110
Position 100. Elephant	111
Position 101. Congress of a Cow	112
Position 102. The 'Quickie'	113

Position 103. Freestanding Love	114
Position 104. Late Spring Donkey	115
Position 105. 9th Posture	116
Position 106. Loving Gaze	117
Position 107. Standing Spontaneity	118

STANDING POSITIONS

Position 108. Bamboo	121
Position 109. Belly to Belly	122
Position 110. Driving the Peg Home	123
Position 111. Standing Split	124
Position 112. Supported Congress	125
Position 113. Suspended Congress	126
Position 114. Weeping Willow	127
Position 115. Wheelbarrow	128

SIDE ON POSITIONS

Position 116. Transverse Lute	131
Position 117. Cicada to the Side	132
Position 118. Mandarin Ducks	133
Position 119. Two Fishes	134
Position 120. 5th Posture	135

MISCELLANEOUS POSITIONS

Position 121. Autumn Dog	139
Position 122. Fitter-In	140
Position 123. Drawing the Bow	141
Position 124. Scissors	142
Position 125. Sitting on Top of the World	143
Position 126. Seagulls on the Wing	144

BONUS - ORAL POSITIONS

All For Her	147
Lean Back	148
Riding His Face	149
Sideways 69	150
69 Her On Top	151
69 Him on Top	152
Standing 69	153

References	155
Author Recommendations	157
About Aventuras	159

THANKS FOR YOUR PURCHASE

Did you know you can get FREE chapters of any SF Nonfiction Book you want?

https://offers.SFNonfictionBooks.com/Free-Chapters

You will also be among the first to know of FREE review copies, discount offers, bonus content, and more.

Go to:

https://offers.SFNonfictionBooks.com/Free-Chapters

Thanks again for your support.

INTRODUCTION

What follows are descriptions of many different positions for you to experiment with. They are grouped into similar positions: from behind, man on top, woman on top, etc. Many can be adapted to masturbation, toy play, and anal sex.

While experimenting, consider the following:

- Where the woman's vagina is too big for the man's penis, use positions where she can grip his penis, or where her legs are drawn to her chest to allow for deeper penetration. Positions where her feet are crossed will make her vagina tighter on his penis.
- If the man is too big for the woman, use positions that do not allow him to penetrate too deeply.

MAN ON TOP

Man-on-top positions allow for face-to-face contact, which is highly intimate. They also give the highest percentage of women orgasms, and are the best for inducing pregnancy.

Some of these positions may be uncomfortable for women who are already pregnant, or when men are too heavy for women.

POSITION 1. 1ST POSTURE

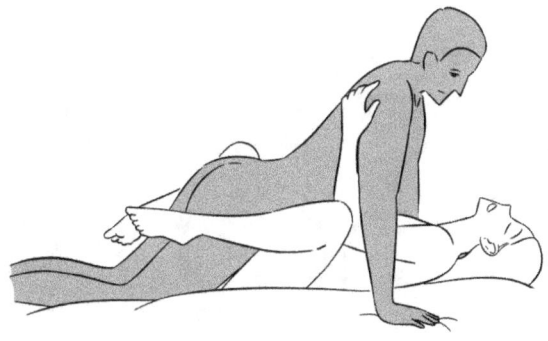

She lies on her back, with her knees pulled back and her legs spread. He lies in between her legs and supports himself on his arms. She can wrap her feet around his thighs. He can enter her at a high angle for clitoral stimulation.

POSITION 2. 2ND POSTURE

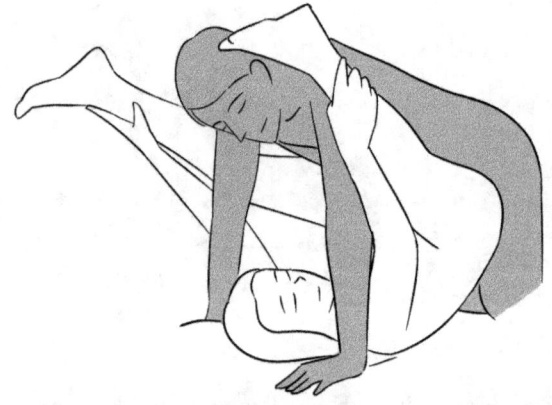

She lies on her back and puts her legs in the air. She grabs her ankles, which opens her up. He rests his weight on his hands, which are placed on either side of her head.

POSITION 3. 3RD POSTURE

He kneels in between her legs. One of her legs goes over his shoulder on the same side (e.g., her right leg on his left shoulder). Her other leg is relaxed near his waist and under his arm.

POSITION 4. 4TH POSTURE

He kneels. She lies on her back and puts her legs on either side of his head. She rests the undersides of her knees on his shoulders.

POSITION 5. BRIDAL BRIDGE

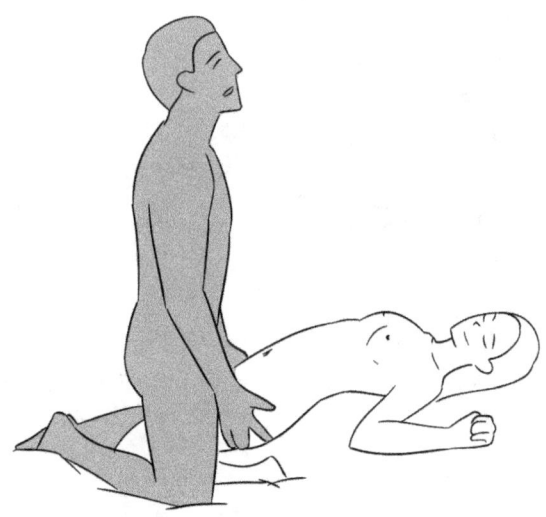

She gets on her knees and lies back onto some pillows. He kneels in front of her, his knees on the outside of hers.

POSITION 6. BACKWARD BENDING FLOWER

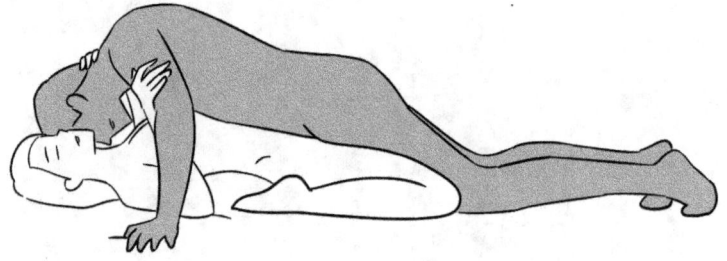

She gets on her knees and lies all the way back. A pillow under her lower back may increase her comfort. He lies on top of her.

POSITION 7. 7TH POSTURE

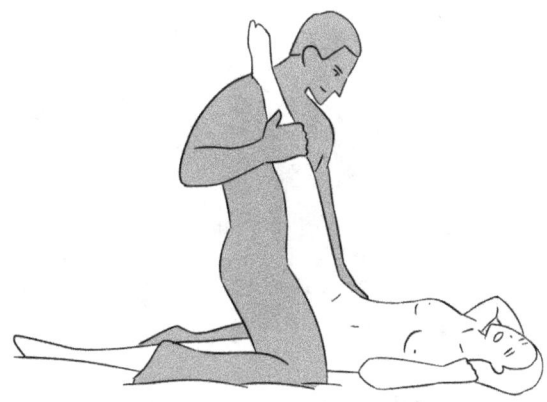

She lies on her back, slightly to one side. He is kneeling. One of her legs is on his shoulder, while the other is straightened underneath him. His knees rest on either side of her grounded leg.

POSITION 8. 8TH POSTURE

She lies on her back with her feet crossed. He is on top, with his knees on either side of her. He supports his weight on his hands and knees.

POSITION 9. APE

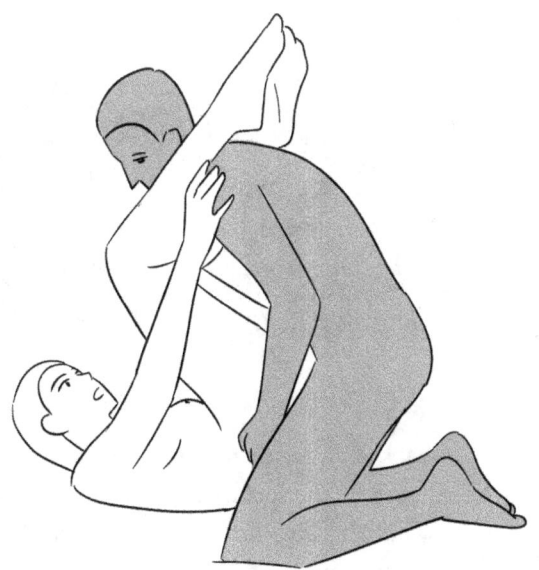

He kneels. She lies on her back and rests her calves on his shoulders. He lifts her by the hips onto his penis.

POSITION 10. 10TH POSTURE

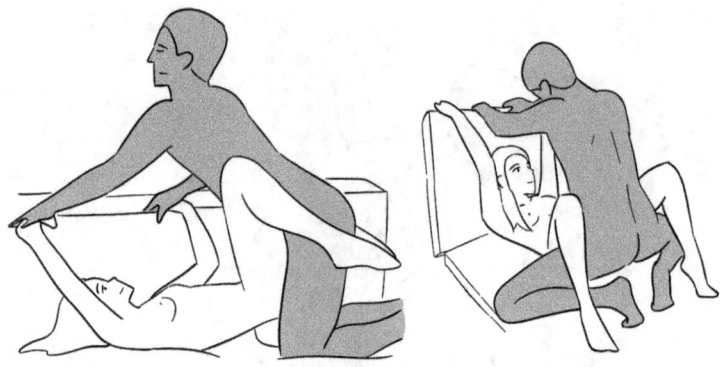

She lies on her back and raises her arms to grab something behind her head, such as the headboard. He is on his knees in between her legs, and he also grabs the headboard. She can raise her hips to meet him or plant her feet on the floor. They can push and pull against whatever they are holding onto.

POSITION 11. 11TH POSTURE

She lies on her back with her legs apart and he lies on top of her, in between her legs. Her feet are on the backs of his calves, and her legs are relaxed. She can press her feet together for a tighter fit.

POSITION 12. LEVEL-FEET

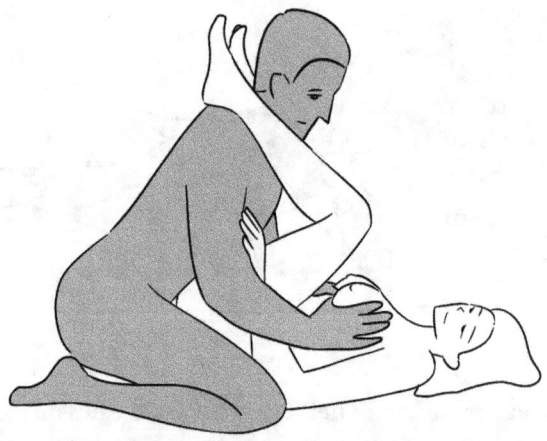

She lies on her back and places her legs on his shoulders, one on either side of his head. He kneels with his legs on either side of her, sitting on his calves.

POSITION 13. PINE TREE

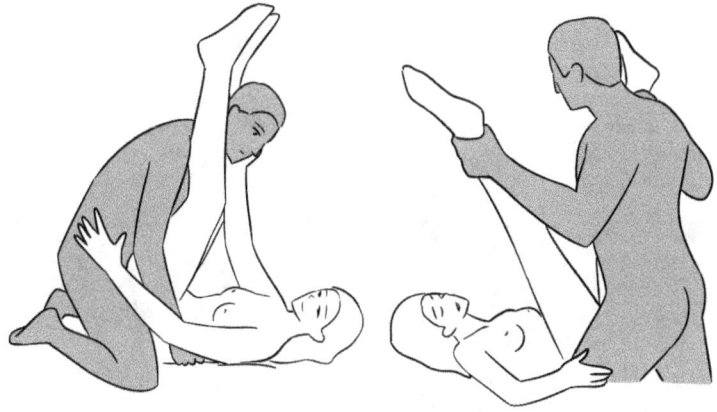

She raises her legs high in the air, one on either side of his head. He kneels up against her. He needs to be careful not to push her legs too far forward. From here, she can spread her legs as he grabs her ankles.

POSITION 14. RISING STAR

She lies on her back, with a pillow under the small of it. She brings her knees to her chest. He kneels in front of her with his knees on either side of her. He leans forward on her, resting his weight on his hands.

POSITION 15. SPLITTING

She lies on her back, with her legs together and in the air. He kneels in front of her, one knee on either side of her. She rests both her legs on one of his shoulders. pressing her knees and thighs together. He can hold her around the knees or come up higher and grab around her calves. She can cross her legs for a tighter fit and he can lean in for deeper penetration.

POSITION 16. TAIL OF THE OSTRICH

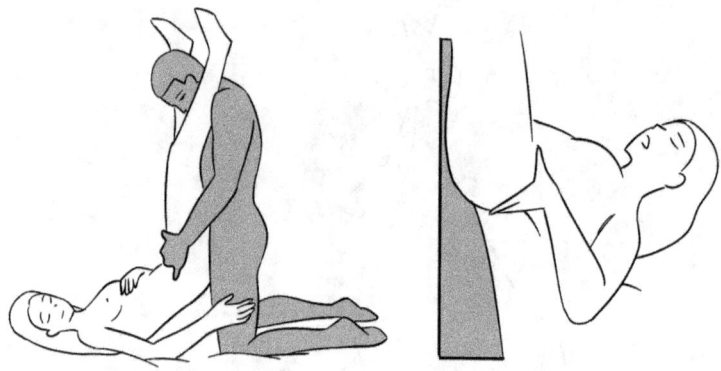

She lies on her back with her legs straight in the air and resting on his shoulders, one on either side of his head. He is on his knees in front of her, in a tall posture. She raises her hips, using her hands if needed.

POSITION 17. SWALLOWS IN LOVE

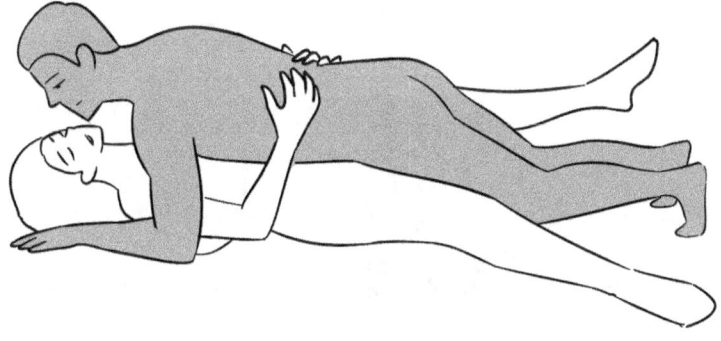

She lies on her back completely flat and relaxed, with her legs slightly apart and fairly straight. He is on top, with his legs in between hers. He rests on his elbows.

POSITION 18. YAWNING

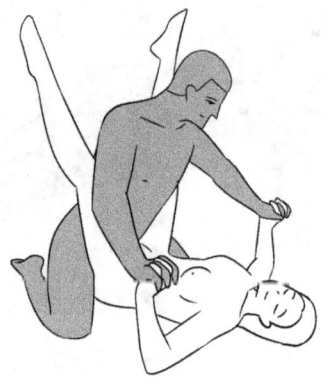

She lies on her back, with her feet high in the air and her legs open. He kneels in between her legs and they join hands. Her legs are at his waist level. He must be careful not to thrust too hard. She can invite deeper penetration by bringing her knees to her chest.

As a variation, she rests her legs on his shoulders and they place their hands on the floor on either side of her head.

He can also lean in closer and she can hold his waist.

POSITION 19. DRAGON TURNS AWAY

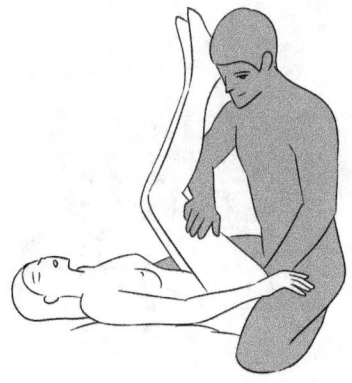

She lies on her back with her legs in the air. He moves them to one side and kneels, with one knee on either side of her.

POSITION 20. G-SPOT STIMULATOR

She lies on her back and places her legs on his shoulders, one on either side of his head. He is on his knees up against her. She raises her buttocks so he can enter her.

POSITION 21. CRAB

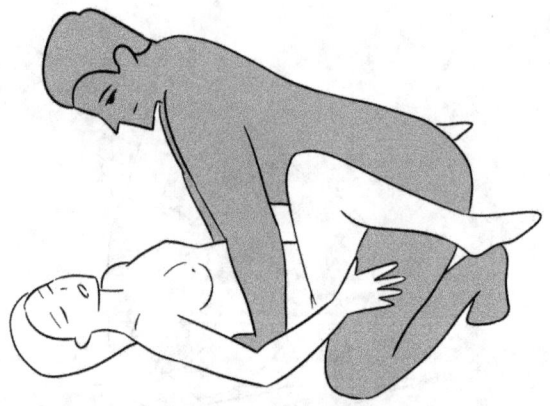

She lies on her back and bends her knees so her feet are off the floor. He kneels, with his knees on either side of her body, and supports his weight on his hands.

POSITION 22. DRAGON TURN

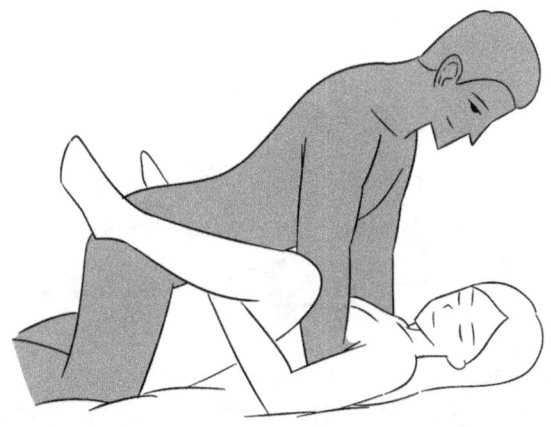

She lies on her back, draws her knees towards her chest, and uses her hands to pull them apart. He is on his knees, with his body in between her legs, and places his knees on either side of her buttocks. He rests his weight on his hands and knees.

POSITION 23. GALLOPING HORSE

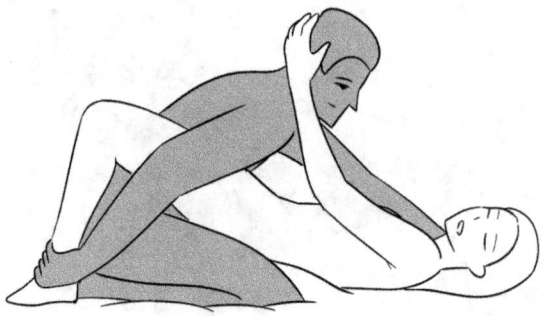

She lies on her back with her feet planted on the floor. He kneels in between her legs. She raises her hips onto him. He holds her by the ankle and the neck.

POSITION 24. GAPING

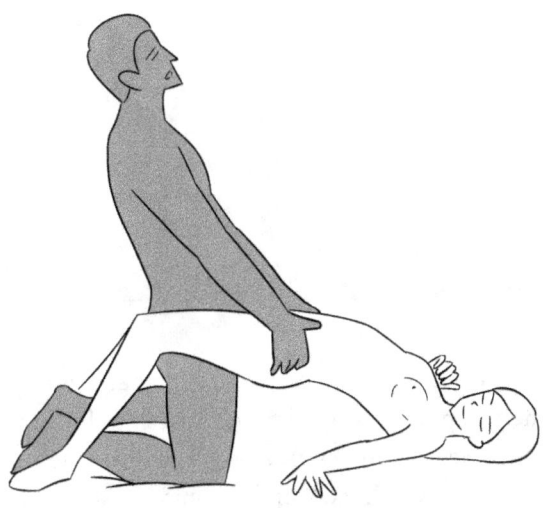

She is on her back. He kneels between her legs. She arches her back to meet his groin and can continue to move her hips up to meet his thrusts. Only her head, arms, the tops of her shoulders, and her feet touch the floor.

POSITION 25. GRIPPING WITH TOES

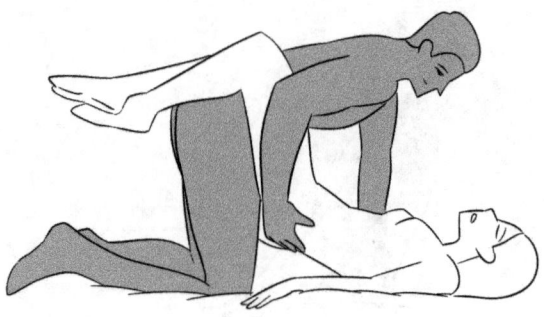

She lies on her back. He kneels in between her legs and uses his arms to help support his weight. She raises her hips to meet his groin and crosses her ankles around his waist, so she can use her legs to raise and lower herself on his penis.

POSITION 26. HUGE BIRD ABOVE A RED SEA

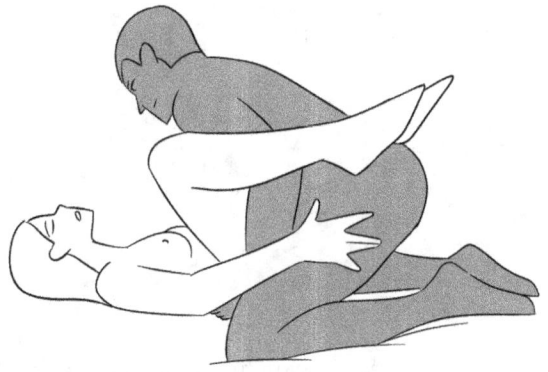

She lies on her back and draws her knees towards her chest. He kneels in between her legs. Her legs go over his arms. He leans forward and raises her buttocks to his groin.

POSITION 27. ONE WHO STOPS AT HOME

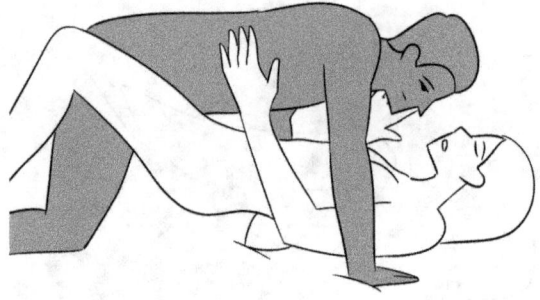

She lies on her back, with him on his knees between her legs. He helps support his weight on his hands. She lifts her pelvis up and down on his penis.

POSITION 28. PLACID EMBRACE

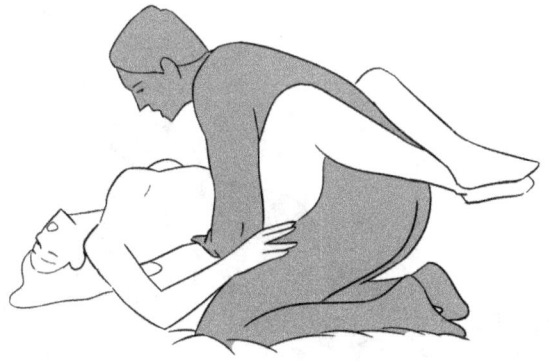

She lies on her back and he kneels in between her legs. He pulls her up onto his groin and she crosses her legs around his back. She pulls him in with her legs and he helps to support her weight with his arms.

POSITION 29. PRESSING

She is on her back and he lies in between her legs, using his arms to support himself. She grips him with her thighs, tightening her vaginal muscles on his penis.

POSITION 30. RAISED FEET

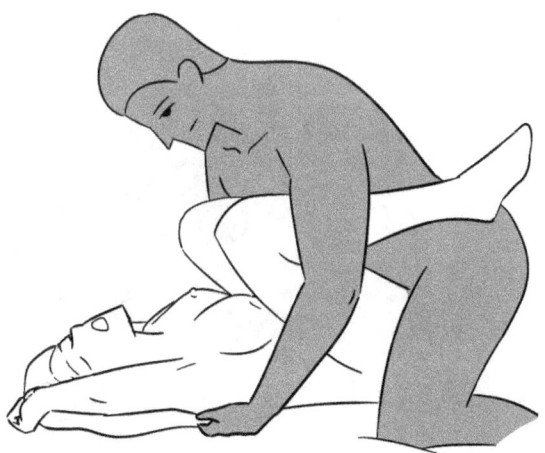

Lying on her back, she bends her legs at the knees and draws them back. He enters her from a kneeling position. They can enhance this position by placing some cushions under her bum. She can pull him closer with her legs.

POSITION 31. REFINED POSITION

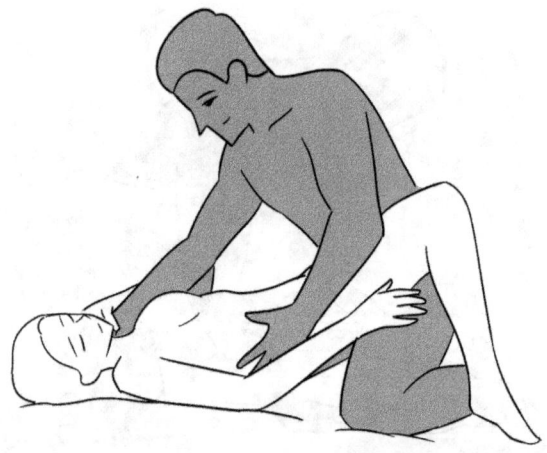

She lies on her back and he kneels in between her legs. Her feet are planted on the floor. She raises her hips to meet his groin.

POSITION 32. SILKWORM SPINNING A COCOON

She is flat on her back and he lies in between her legs, supporting his weight on his hands. She wraps her legs tightly around his torso, then raises and lowers her hips in time with his thrusts.

POSITION 33. STOPPERAGE

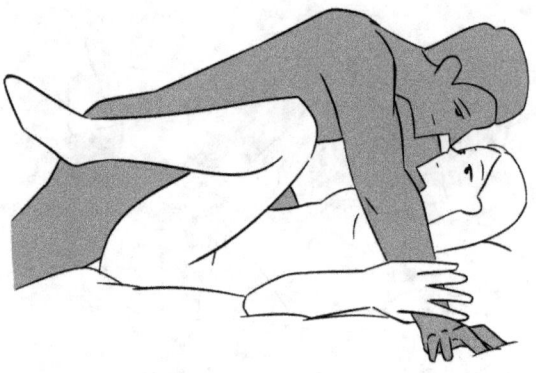

She lies on her back and brings her knees towards her chest. He kneels between her legs, bringing his face close to hers while supporting his weight on his hands. She can draw him in by pressing her heels on his buttocks.

POSITION 34. TWINING

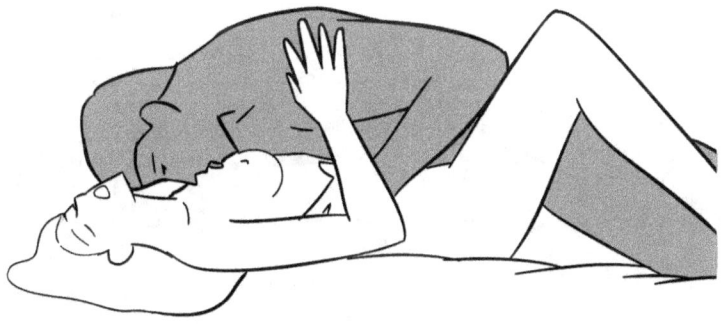

He lies in between her legs. She hooks her legs around the top of his thighs.

POSITION 35. CLASPING

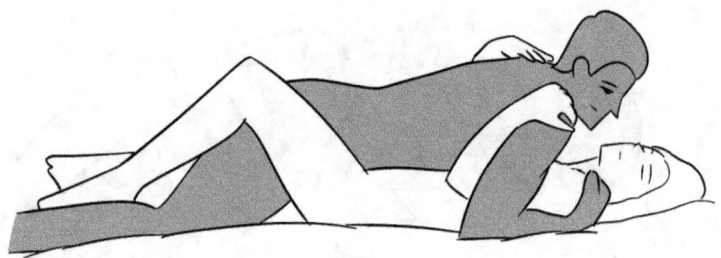

He lies on top, with his legs in between hers. Her feet wrap over his legs and rest on the inside.

POSITION 36. FIXING A NAIL

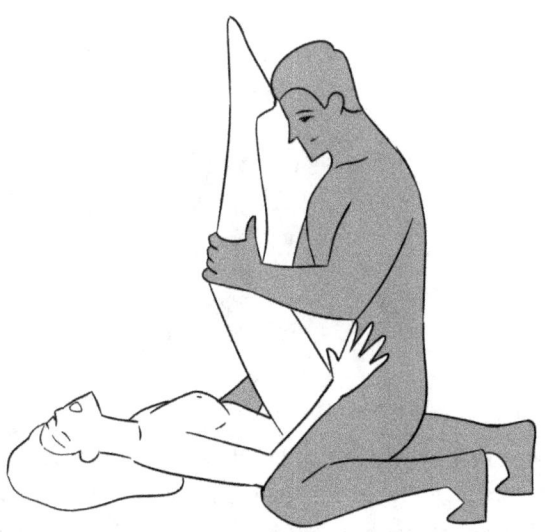

He kneels up close to her. One of her legs is raised, with her heel at his forehead. From there, he can massage her calf and thigh with one hand, while playing with her clitoris or anus with the other. She can vary the sensations by moving her leg.

POSITION 37. HALF PRESSED

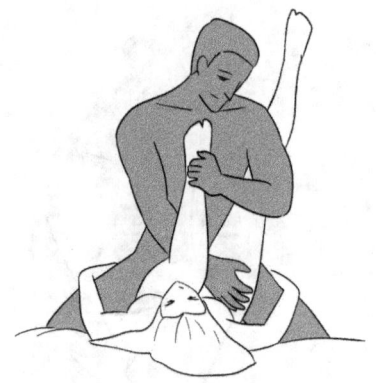

She raises her knees to her chest. He kneels up close to her with his legs spread. One of her legs stretches past his waist and under his arm. Her other foot is placed on his chest. She grabs him by the thighs and he holds her thigh and foot. He should keep his buttocks relaxed and can massage her foot. She can caress his buttocks and thighs and move her hips on him.

POSITION 38. HORSE SHAKES FEET

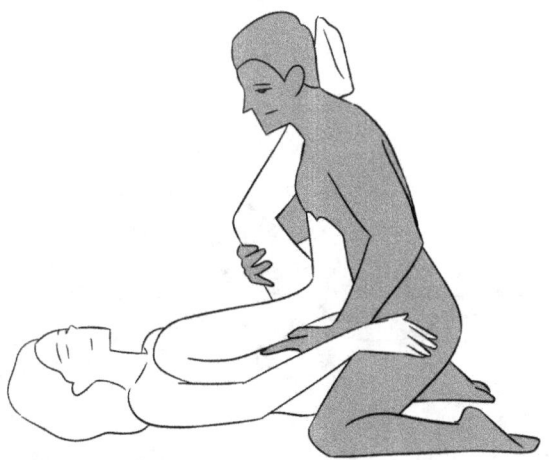

She draws her knees to her chest. He kneels up close, with his knees on either side of her body. One of her legs goes over his shoulder, while her other foot can rest on his stomach or chest. She can shake her raised foot as he thrusts.

POSITION 39. SPLITTING OF BAMBOO

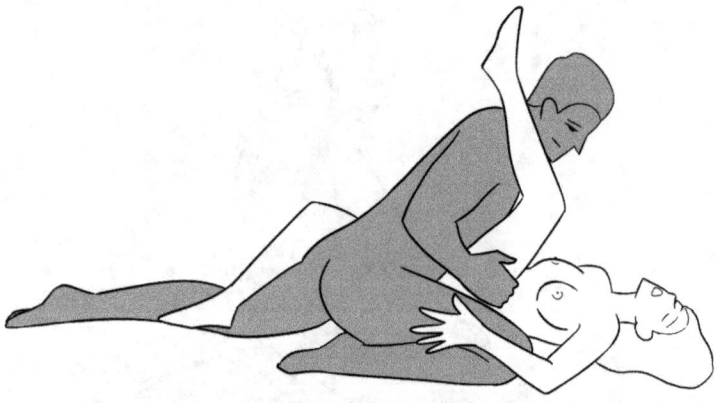

He is up against her on one knee. That knee is on the outside of her torso. His other leg is stretched back. Her leg that is on the same side as his bent knee is on his shoulder. Her other leg wraps around his outstretched leg. She swaps the position of her legs throughout intercourse.

POSITION 40. ANKLE HOLD

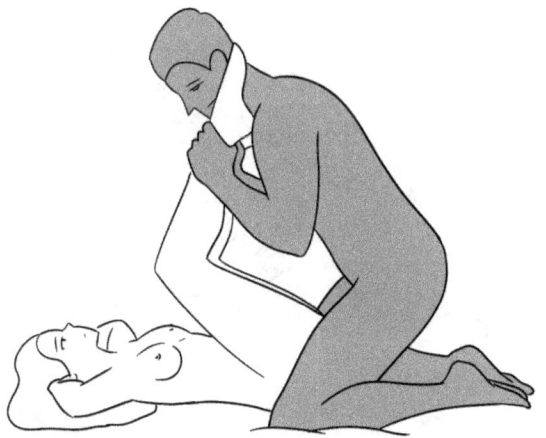

He grabs her by the ankles, with his knees on either side of her buttocks. He holds her feet near his face.

POSITION 41. FETAL FLOWER

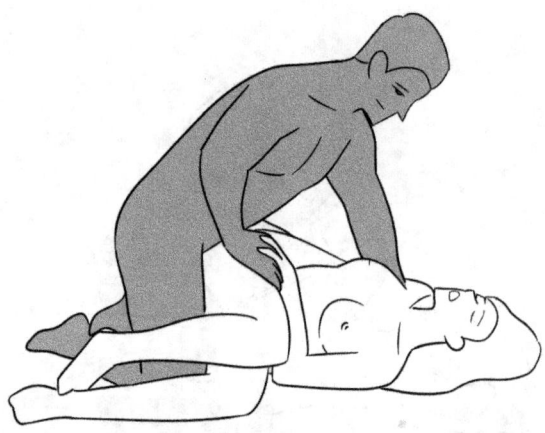

She bends her legs at the knees and leans them to one side. He kneels up against her, behind her legs. She can move her legs in a cyclic motion.

POSITION 42. ENCIRCLING

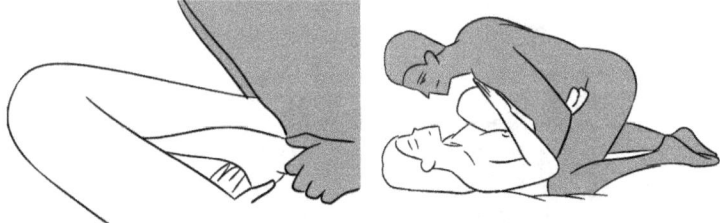

She brings her feet to her chest and crosses her calves. He kneels, with his feet on either side of her body, and leans toward her.

POSITION 43. HELD FEET

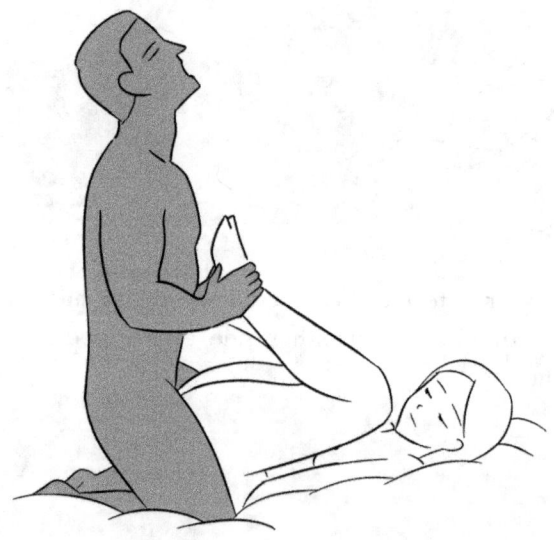

He grabs her by the feet and kneels, with a knee on either side of her. He brings her feet together and pushes her knees to her chest. He can massage her feet.

POSITION 44. HORSE CROSS FEET

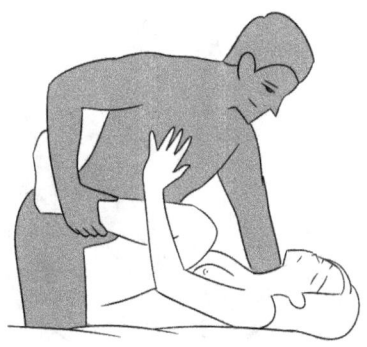

He kneels with his knees on either side of her body. He grabs one of her ankles and pushes her knee to her chest. He uses his other hand to help support himself. As he thrusts, he pumps her leg.

POSITION 45. INTACT POSTURE

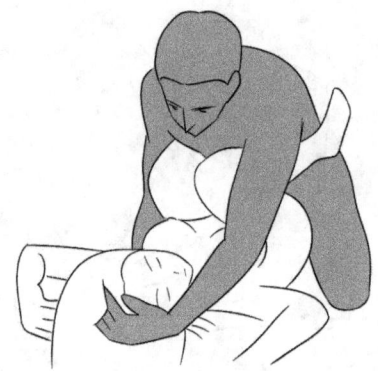

She brings her knees to her chest and keeps them close together. He is on his knees and presses into her, with his chest on her knees. They should start gently.

POSITION 46. JADE JOINT

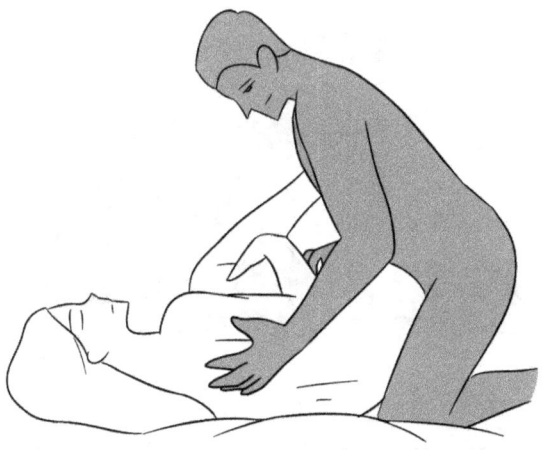

She lies on her side and brings her upper knee to her chest, with her bottom leg straight. She uses her hand to help pull it into position. He kneels with one knee at her back and the other wherever it feels comfortable.

POSITION 47. JOINING THE LOTUS

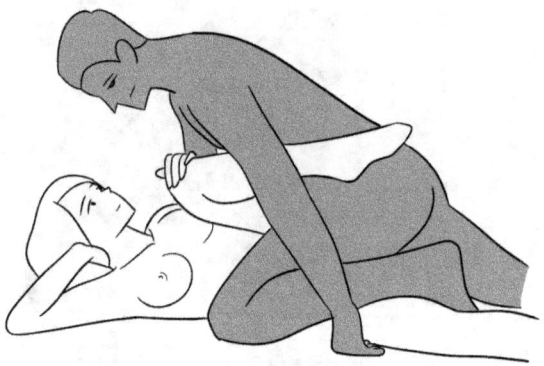

She lies on one side, supporting her head with her hand. She uses her hand to bring her top knee to her chest. Her other leg is laid out flat. He puts his knee between her legs, resting it in front of her body. His foot rests on the thigh of her extended leg. His other leg is stretched out behind him. Her raised calf is between his torso and arm.

POSITION 48. LOTUS

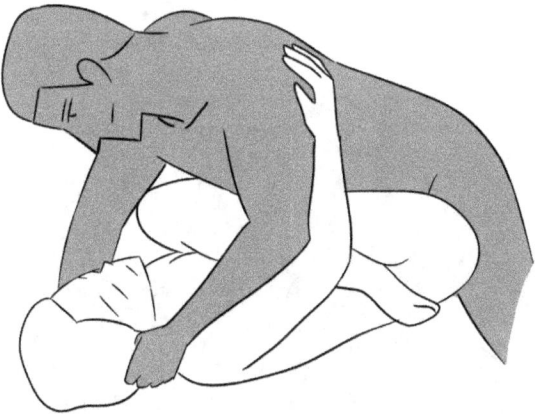

She crosses her ankles and draws her knees up. He kneels with his knees on either side of her and leans over her, resting on his hands. He can lean into her legs if she is flexible enough.

POSITION 49. MANDARIN DUCK

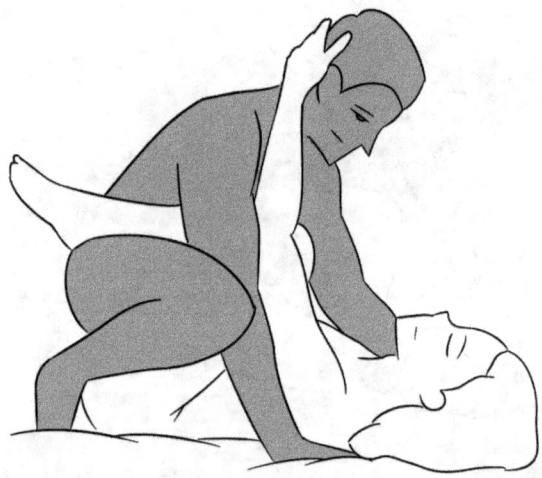

She brings one of her knees to her chest and stretches her other leg out. He squats over her, with his feet on either side of her body. Her raised calf rests on his thigh. He uses his hands to support himself.

POSITION 50. PHOENIX PLAYING IN A RED CAVE

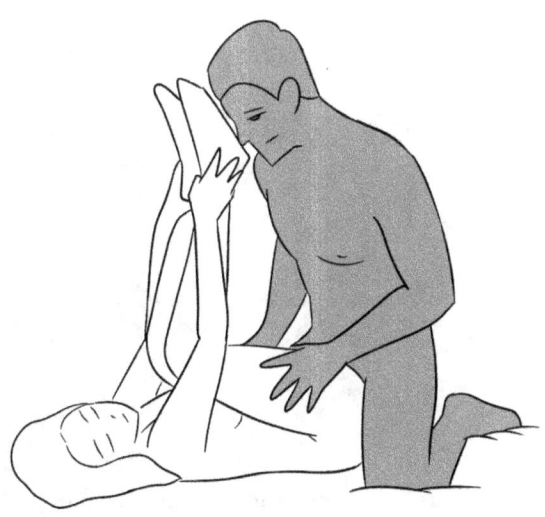

She brings her knees to her chest and holds her ankles together. He kneels with his knees on either side of her.

POSITION 51. PRESSED

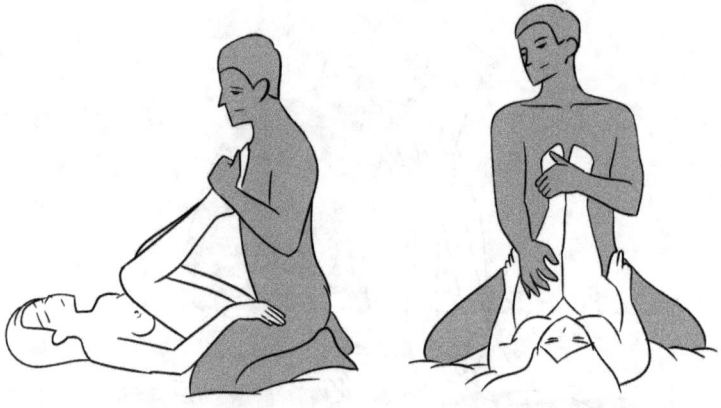

He kneels with his knees on either side of her. She places both her feet on his chest. He massages her feet as he thrusts.

POSITION 52. PUMPING THE WELL

He is in a lunge position. She raises her hips to meet his groin. Her leg, on the same side as his bent leg, is slanted up his torso, so her foot is near his head. He presses his torso against this leg as he thrusts. Her other leg is bent at the knee, with her foot pointing to the sky.

POSITION 53. TURNING

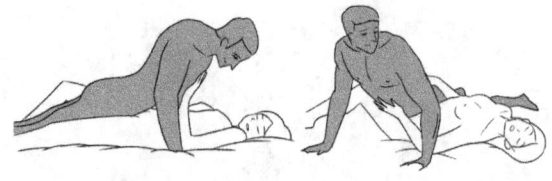

He lies on top of her. Without taking his penis out, he turns 90 degrees, lifting his legs over hers until their bodies are at right angles. She supports his body with her hands to make the turn easier.

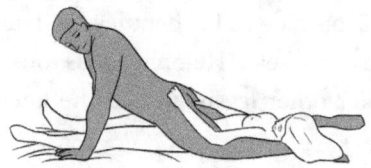

He continues to turn in the same direction until he is facing her feet, with his legs on either side of her body. Using lots of lubrication will make the turn easier.

POSITION 54. RISING

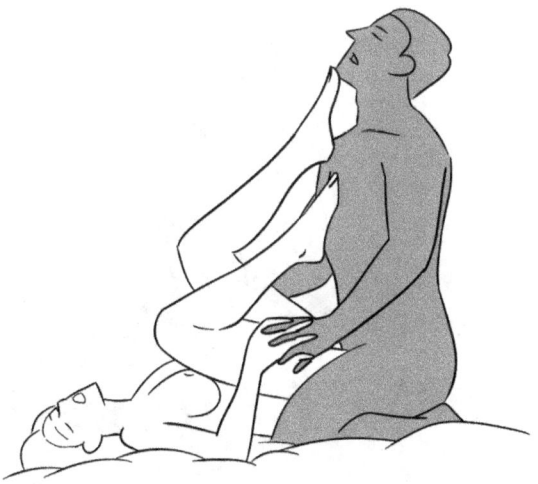

He kneels with his knees on either side of her. She raises her knees towards her chest. One foot is near his shoulder, while the other is on his chest.

POSITION 55. TURTLE MOVE

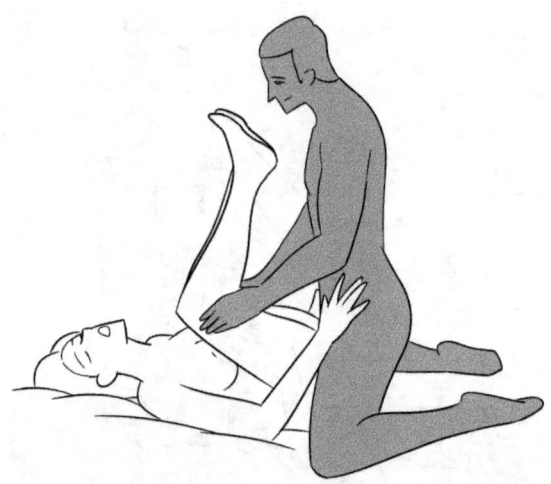

He kneels with his knees on either side of her. She brings her knees to her chest and he keeps her legs together by holding her at her knees. He almost withdraws his penis on every thrust.

POSITION 56. WIFE OF INDRA

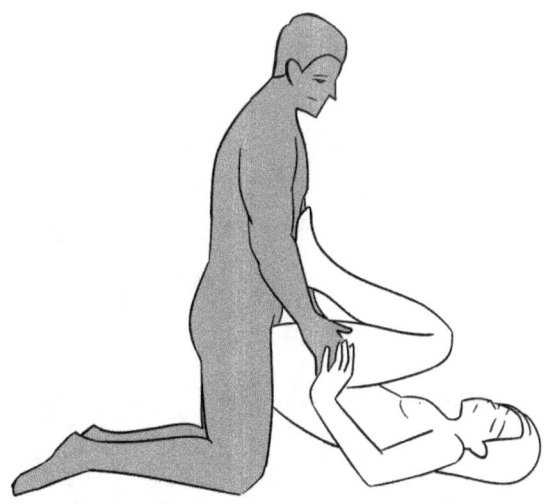

He kneels with his legs close together. She also has her legs together, and raises her hips to meet his groin. Her feet are on his stomach or chest.

WOMAN ON TOP

Positions where the woman is on top enable her to have more control. The man should embrace the submissive feeling.

POSITION 57. BUTTERFLIES IN FLIGHT

She lies on top of him. They are both flat. Her legs are on his legs and her chest is on his chest. They hold hands outstretched to their sides. He flexes his feet and she pushes against them to slide up and down on his body.

She can raise her leg to get more of a push if she needs to.

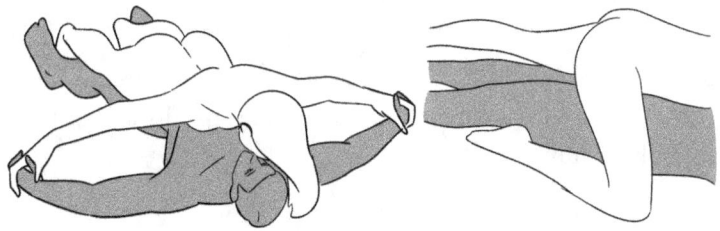

POSITION 58. FISH

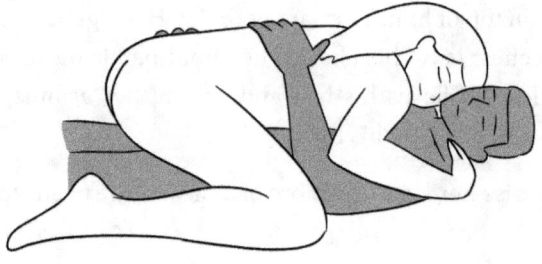

She straddles him, with her knees on either side of his torso. Her chest is pressed against his. She can move vertically and/or horizontally on him.

POSITION 59. INTERCHANGE OF COITION

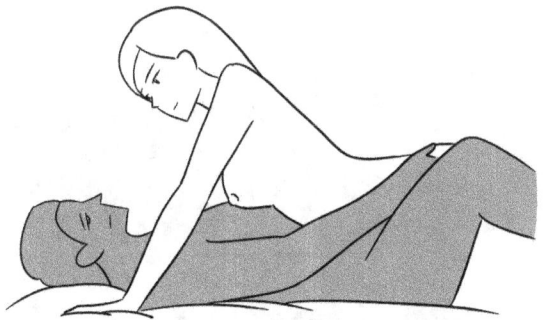

He raises his knees a little and spreads them apart. She lies in between his legs, supporting herself with her hands.

POSITION 60. INVERTED EMBRACE

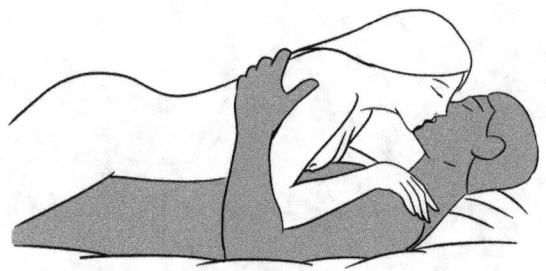

She lies flat on top of him. Their legs are together.

POSITION 61. SHARING REINS

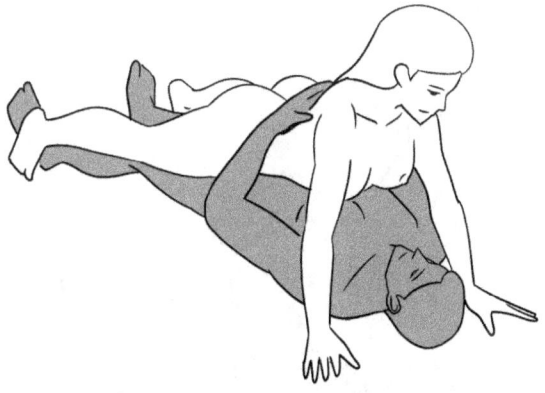

With their legs slightly spread, she lays on top of him. She supports her weight on her hands, which are placed on either side of his head. She pushes to raise her chest off his.

POSITION 62. ACCOMPLISHING POSITION

He sits cross-legged. She sits on him and leans back on one hand. She raises one leg in the air while planting her other foot on the floor.

POSITION 63. ALTERNATIVE MOVEMENT OF PIERCING

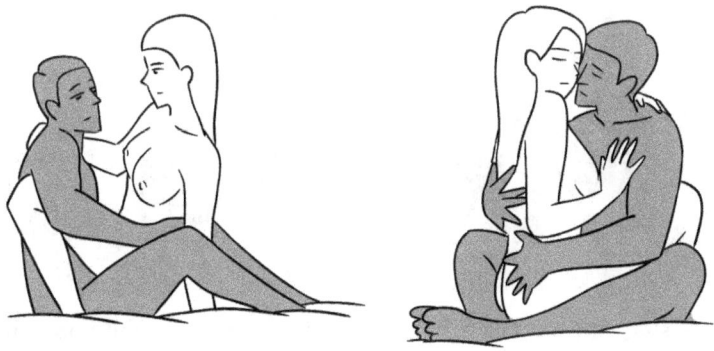

He sits with the soles of his feet together. She sits in between his legs, with her legs on the outside of his hips and her feet planted on the floor. She leans back on one hand and uses the other to grab his shoulder. Alternatively, she can sit close to him with her feet off or on the floor.

POSITION 64. FROG FASHION

He sits with his knees raised and feet planted on the floor. He leans back onto his hands. She sits in the same position, with one leg in between his legs. Their legs alternate. Their feet are placed on the outside of each other's bodies.

From here, he can hold onto her if she wants to lean back.

POSITION 65. KAMA'S WHEEL

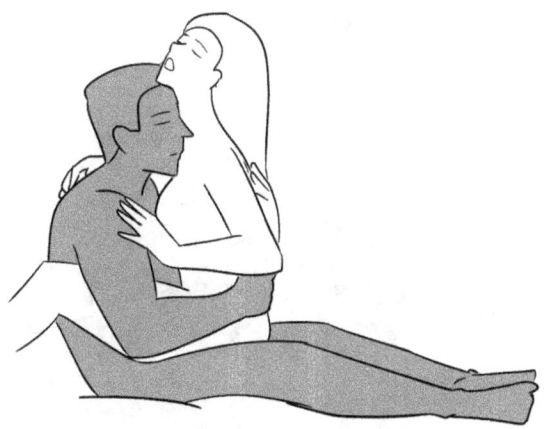

He sits with his legs stretched out. She straddles him, with a leg on either side of him.

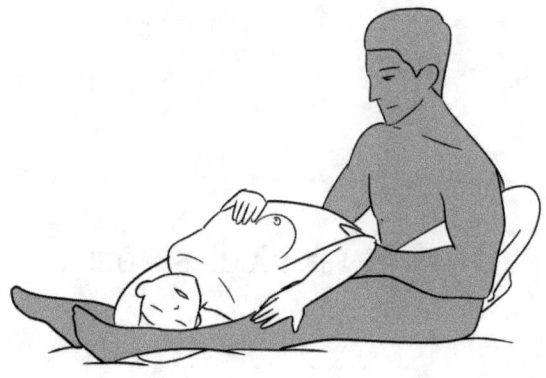

Their upper bodies can be close together or she can lean back.

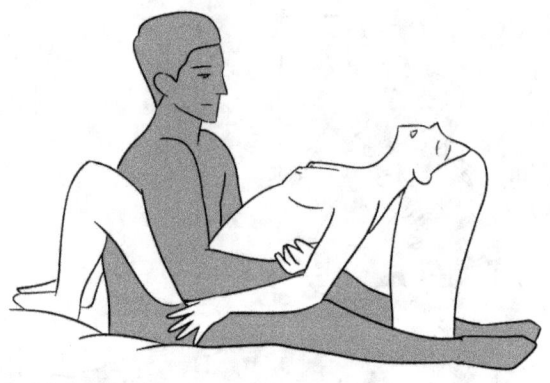

She moves herself up and down or in circles.

POSITION 66. CRYING OUT

He sits with his legs out and she straddles him. Her legs are slung over his arms and he grabs her waist. She can use her hand behind her for support.

POSITION 67. LOTUS INVERTED

He sits crossed-legged. She straddles him, with her feet planted behind him. They hug close and he lifts her up and down on himself. She can also take some weight on her feet. From here, he can lie down while she moves, or she can lean back on her hands and rock back and forth.

POSITION 68. LOVING LIFT

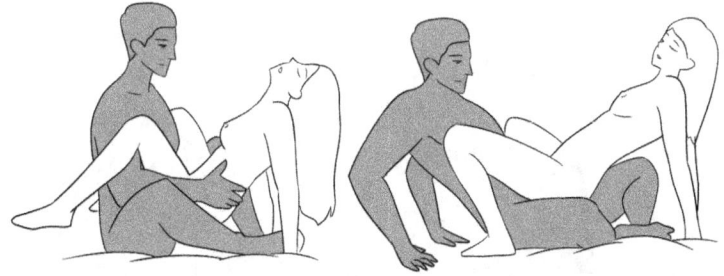

He sits with the soles of his feet together. She sits inside his legs with her feet on either side of his body. Her legs go over his arms at the elbows and he holds her waist. She leans back, supporting her weight on her hands. He closes his thighs slightly to help support her. He moves her on him.

If he gets tired, she can put her feet on the floor and rock on him while he leans back.

POSITION 69. PAIRED FEET

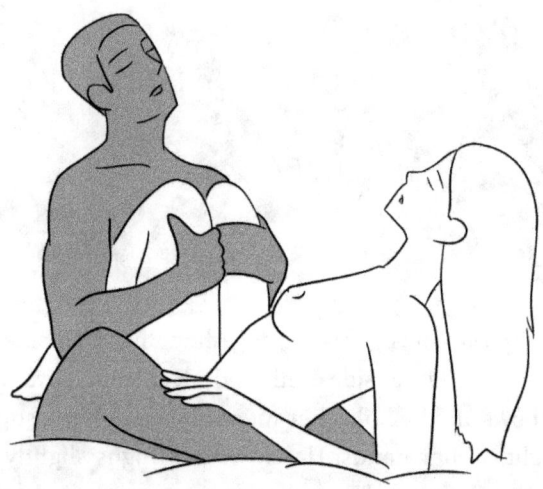

He sits with his legs wide apart. She sits on him, with her feet on either side of him. She leans back and he brings her knees together.

POSITION 70. POSITION OF EQUALS

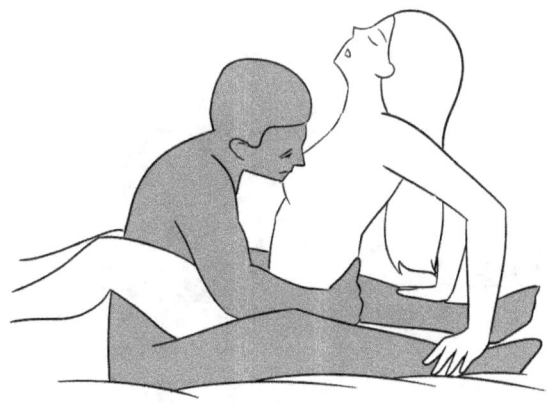

He sits with his legs stretched out in front of him. She sits between his legs with her legs crossed around his torso in the air. She leans back, placing her hands on his ankles.

POSITION 71. SINGING MONKEY

He sits with his legs stretched out in front of him. She sits between his legs, with her legs crossed around his torso and her feet planted on the floor. Their chests are close together. She can lean back on her hand to thrust on him.

POSITION 72. SNAKE TRAP

He sits with his legs stretched out in front of him. She sits between his legs, with her legs on either side of his torso and her feet planted on the floor. They both lean back, holding each other's feet for support as they rock.

POSITION 73. YIN AND YANG

This is also known as Yab Yum. He sits cross-legged and she sits on top of him. They hold each other close and she crosses her legs around his back.

POSITION 74. ASCENDING POSITION

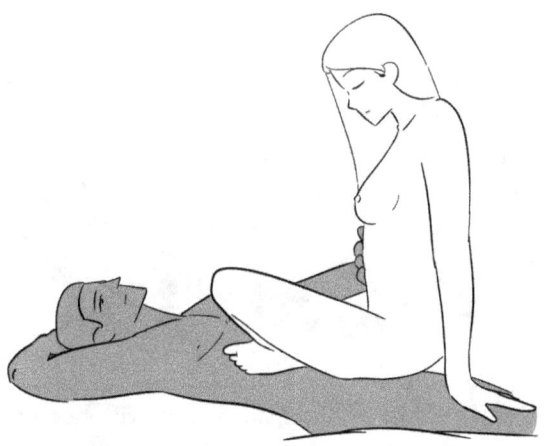

He lies down flat and she sits on him with crossed legs.

POSITION 75. BUTTERFLY

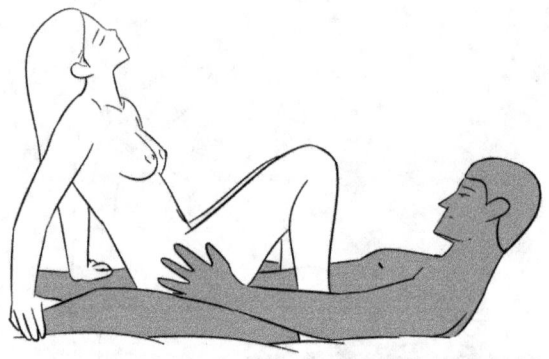

He lies flat on his back and she sits on him with her feet planted on either side of his torso. She leans back and holds his legs. If she gets tired, she can go to her knees.

POSITION 76. CAT AND MOUSE SHARING A HOLE

He lies flat on his back with his legs close together. She lies on top of him with her legs on the outside of his. She supports her weight with her arms.

POSITION 77. CATBIRD SEAT

He lies on his back and she kneels over him, a knee on either side of his body. She bends over him so that they are parallel to each other. She can lean forward to get more clitoral stimulation or lean back to hit the G-spot.

POSITION 78. LOVE SEAT

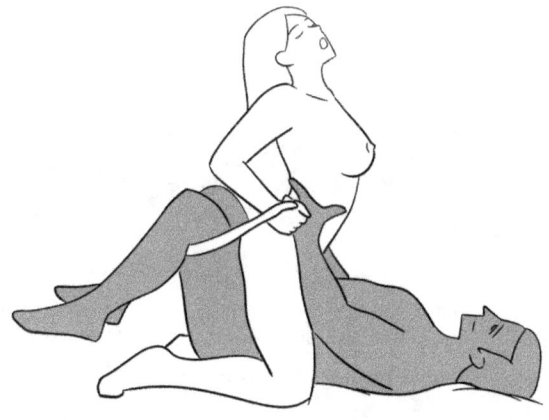

He lies on his back and she sits on top of him, with a knee on either side of his body. He lifts his knees towards her buttocks. She can use some material such as a scarf, to gain more leverage. She can put her feet flat on the floor and lean back into his thighs.

POSITION 79. ORGASMIC ROLE-REVERSAL

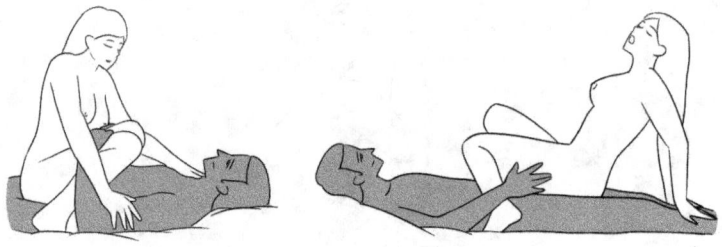

He lies on his back and she squats on him, a foot on either side of his body. He holds her legs together.

For a change of angle, she can lean back and hold his legs.

POSITION 80. PAIR OF TONGS

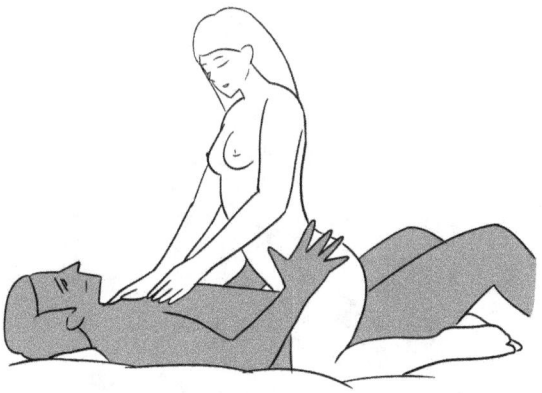

He lies on his back and she sits on top of him, with a knee on either side of his torso. She clasps his hips between her thighs, then slides up and down and forward and backward. She can push his thighs together with her feet.

POSITION 81. RACE OF THE MEMBER

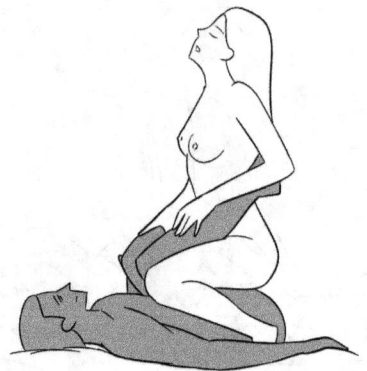

He lies on his back and draws his knees to his chest. She squats on him, with her feet on either side of his buttocks. Her knees are on the outside of his knees. His legs come over her thighs and under her arms.

POSITION 82. HANGING BOW

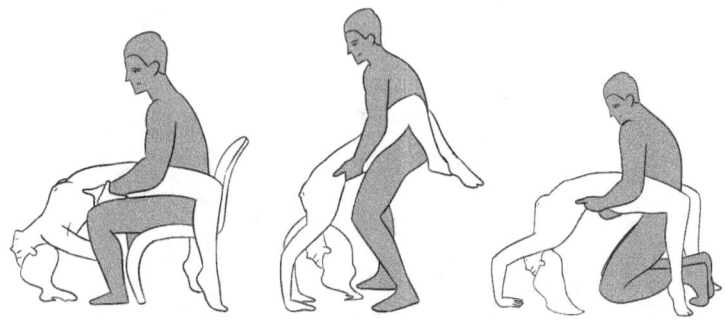

He sits on a chair and she straddles him. He supports her lower back and she grabs his wrists as she arches back. Her legs dangle, relaxed. She then places her hands on the floor and he slowly stands. She crosses her feet behind him.

Finally, he lowers himself down to his knees. Her feet may touch the floor.

POSITION 83. SPIDER

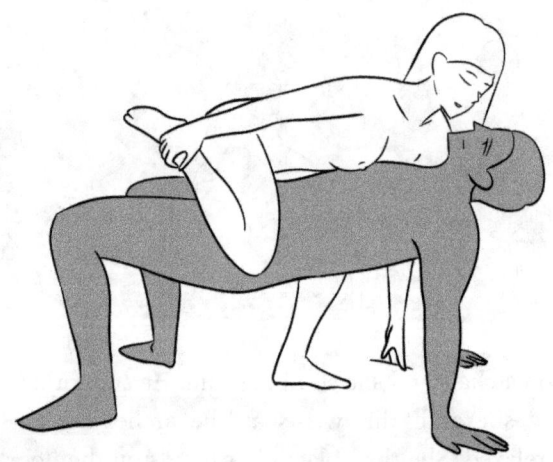

He raises himself on his hands and feet, facing the ceiling. She straddles him, keeping at least one foot planted firmly on the floor.

POSITION 84. GOAT AND THE TREE

He sits on a chair and she sits on top of him, facing away from him.

POSITION 85. MARE

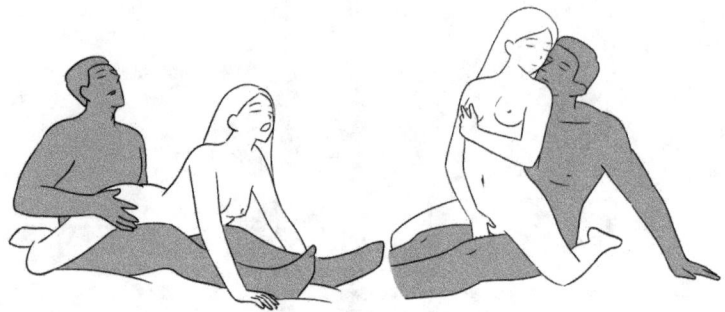

He sits with his legs stretched out in front of him. She faces away from him and sits on him. Her knees are on either side of his hips, with her feet behind him. She bends forward and supports herself on her hands, which are on either side of his feet. She uses her vaginal muscles to milk his penis.

She can sit up straight and stimulate her clitoris.

POSITION 86. RABBIT GROOMING

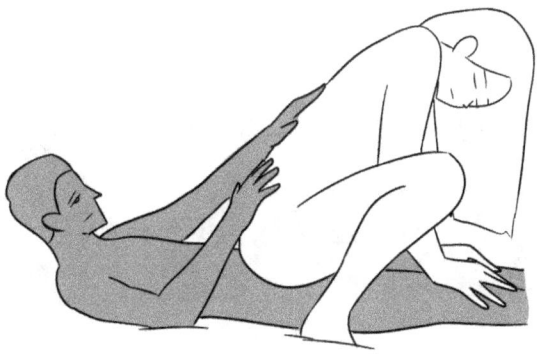

He lies on his back and she squats onto him with her legs on the outside of his legs, facing away from him. If she gets tired, she can switch to a kneeling position.

POSITION 87. RECIPROCAL SIGHTS OF THE POSTERIORS

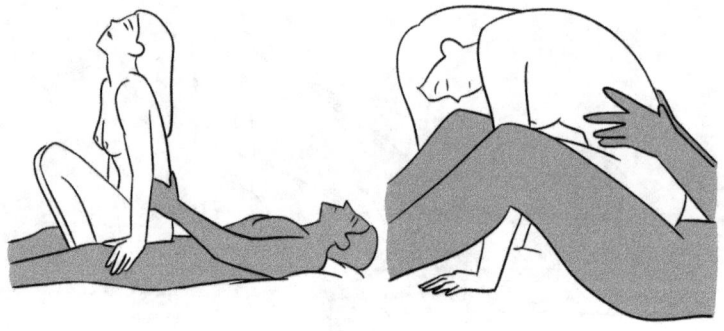

He lies on his back and she squats onto him with her legs between his. She is facing away from him. She can lean forward for an erotic view.

POSITION 88. REVERSE CRAB

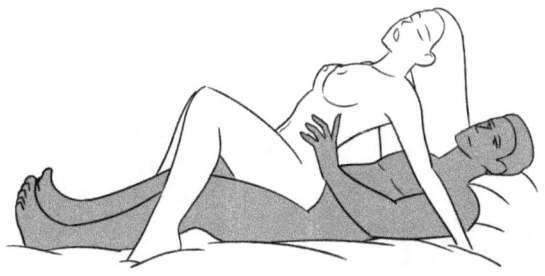

He lies on his back and she sits on him, facing away from him. Her feet are on either side of his legs. She leans back on her hands, which are planted on either side of him.

POSITION 89. SWING

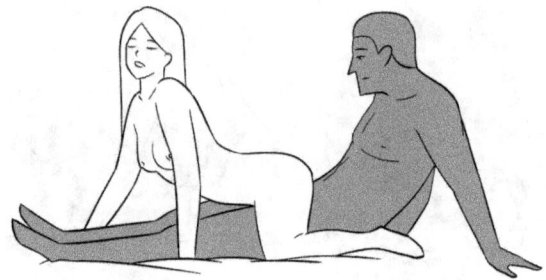

He sits with his legs stretched out in front of him and leans back onto his hands. Facing away from him, she gets on her hands and knees, which are placed on the outside of his legs. He can run his fingers down her spine while she moves on him.

POSITION 90. SPINNING THE TOP

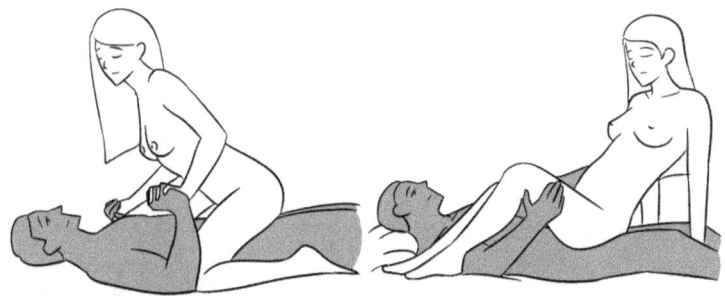

He lies on his back with his legs stretched out in front of him. She straddles him, with her knees on either side of his body. She leans back onto her hands, bringing her feet to the outside of one of his shoulders. They clasp hands for support, and she arches her back. When ready, she continues to spin on him, using her hands to support some of her weight.

She ends up facing away from him, leaning back on her hands, which are placed on his chest. She leans forwards and backwards to experience different sensations.

POSITION 91. TOPPING AND TURNING

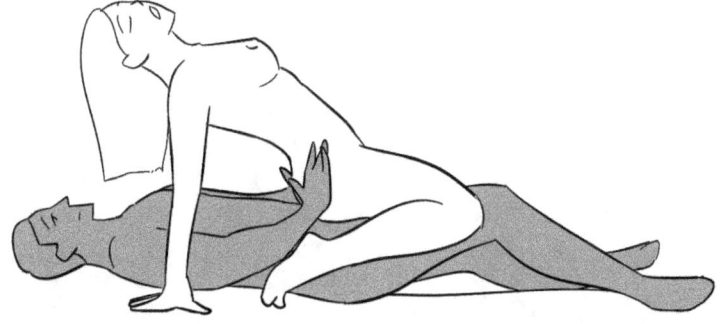

He lies on his back. Facing away from him, she squats on him, with her feet on the outside of his legs. She then leans back onto her hands, which are placed on either side of his shoulders.

FROM BEHIND

Although not as intimate as positions where they are facing each other, a man taking his lover from behind can give great pleasure. It is a highly dominant position for the man.

POSITION 92. 6TH POSTURE (DOGGY STYLE)

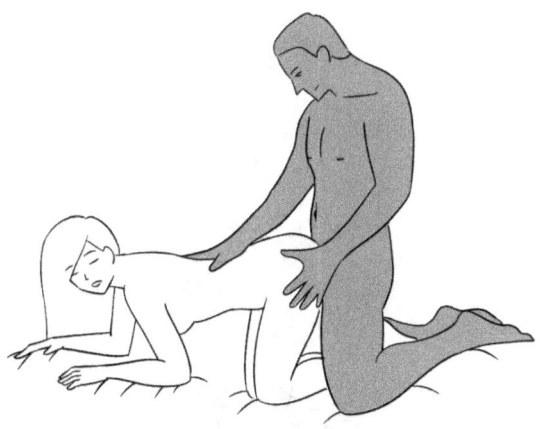

She gets on her hands (or forearms) and knees. He gets on his knees behind her. His knees are on the outside of her legs.

POSITION 93. LOVING CHAIR

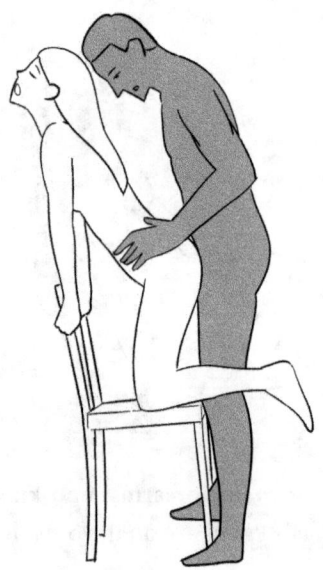

She kneels on a chair facing, the back of it and holds the back for support. He stands behind her.

POSITION 94. RISING PILLOWS

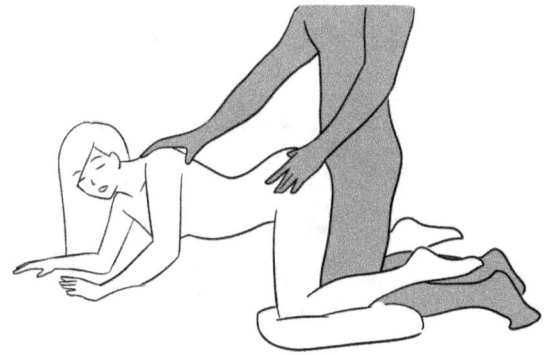

She gets on her knees and relaxes over a mound of pillows that raises her buttocks into the air. Her legs are spread, and he kneels in between them.

POSITION 95. STANDING DOGGY

She gets on her knees in an upright position and spreads her legs a little. He kneels with his knees in between hers. His chest is pressed to her back.

POSITION 96. TIGER STEP

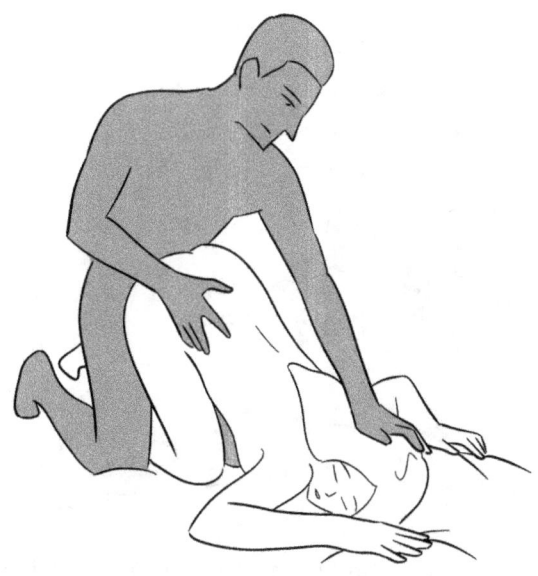

She gets on her knees with her feet crossed and leans forwards, relaxing her head, arms and chest on the floor. Her bum is in the air. He kneels behind her, with his knees on either side of hers.

POSITION 97. WHITE TIGER

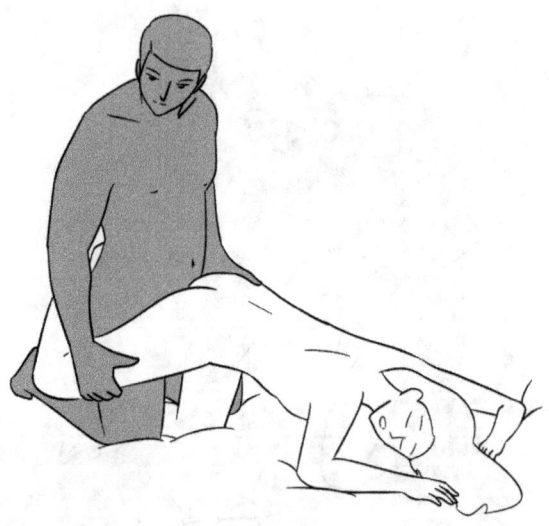

She rests on one knee and her elbows. He kneels with one knee on either side of her grounded knee. He holds her other leg up on the outside of his thigh. She can hook her raised leg around his buttocks.

POSITION 98. CICADA ON A BOUGH

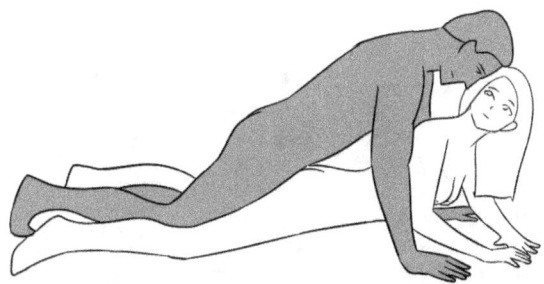

She lies on her stomach, with her legs spread. He lies on top of her, with his legs in between hers. He supports himself on his hands. She can do the same.

POSITION 99. COITUS FROM BEHIND

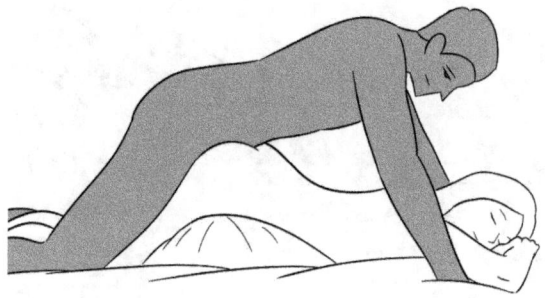

She lies on her stomach, with her legs together and with a cushion under her pelvis to raise her buttocks. He lies on top of her with his legs on either side of hers. He supports himself with his hands on either side of her shoulders.

POSITION 100. ELEPHANT

She lies on her stomach. He lies on top of her, raising his chest by pushing his hands into the floor on either side of her waist.

POSITION 101. CONGRESS OF A COW

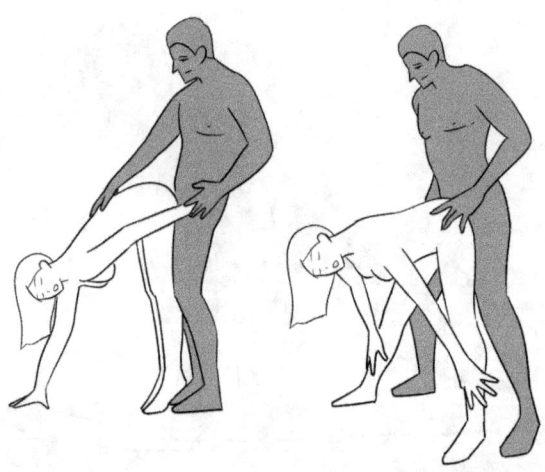

From a standing position, she bends over, placing one or both hands on the floor. Her legs stay straight. He stands behind her and pulls her back and forth onto him. If she is not that flexible, she can put her hands on a raised object such as a chair or the bed. Her legs can be together or apart.

POSITION 102. THE 'QUICKIE'

Although many positions can accommodate the quickie, coming from behind while standing often works the best. Clothes do not even have to be removed, and the man has complete control over his climax.

Note: Quickies are a lot of fun, but don't get addicted, otherwise you'll miss a lot of pleasure.

POSITION 103. FREESTANDING LOVE

She stands with her legs together and squats just a little. He stands behind her.

POSITION 104. LATE SPRING DONKEY

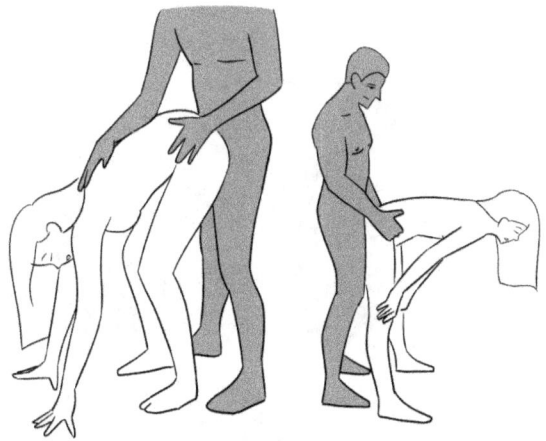

She stands with her legs apart and places both hands on the floor, bending her knees a little. He stands behind her. If she wants, she can straighten her legs and place her hands on her knees.

POSITION 105. 9TH POSTURE

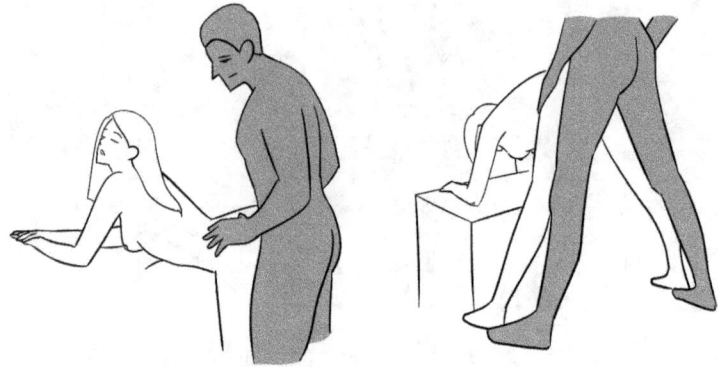

She kneels, facing the edge of the bed or another piece of furniture, and rests her upper body on it. She uses her forearms to prop herself up. He kneels behind her. Alternatively, they can stand.

POSITION 106. LOVING GAZE

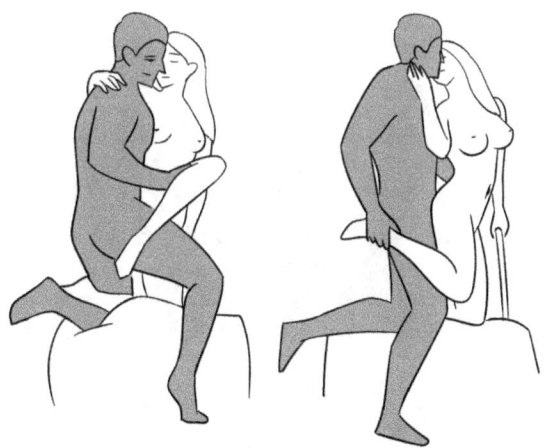

She kneels on the edge of the bed. He comes up behind her, placing one knee on the bed and one foot on the floor. He grabs the leg or foot of hers closest to the edge, and holds it on the outside of the leg on which he is standing. She turns to look at him, which aligns their groins.

POSITION 107. STANDING SPONTANEITY

He comes up behind her. She bends over on any available surface.

STANDING POSITIONS

Some standing positions can be difficult to achieve, as they require more flexibility and/or strength.

POSITION 108. BAMBOO

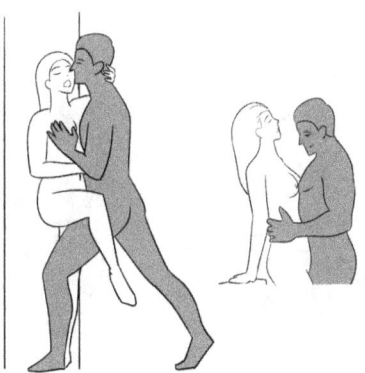

Her back is to a wall and he lunges to her so their chests are close together. She puts her leg over his forward-most leg.

If she is up against something lower (such as a bed or table), she can lean back on her hands while he grabs her around the waist.

POSITION 109. BELLY TO BELLY

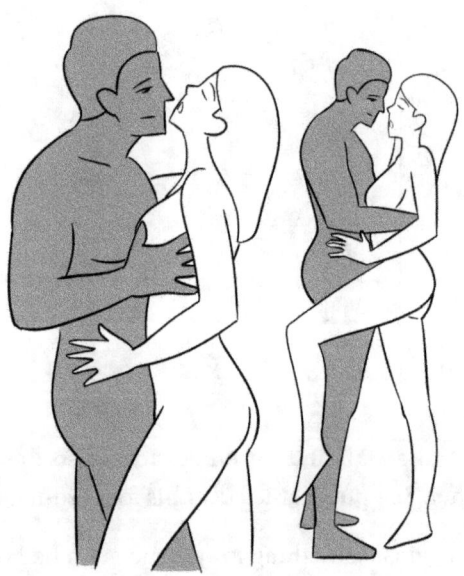

They stand face to face, close against each other. She can hook a leg over his thigh. It will help if she thrusts her pelvis forward.

POSITION 110. DRIVING THE PEG HOME

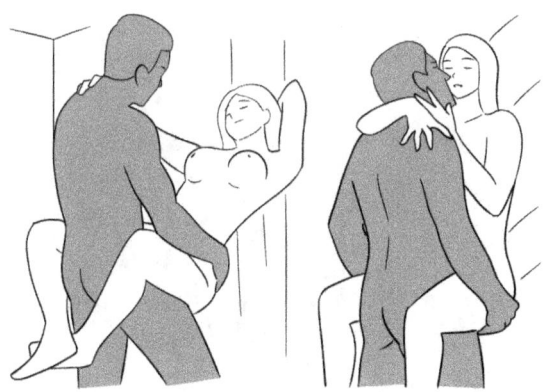

He stands. She wraps her legs around his waist while holding his shoulders. She can lean back into a wall or be pressed tightly against it.

POSITION 111. STANDING SPLIT

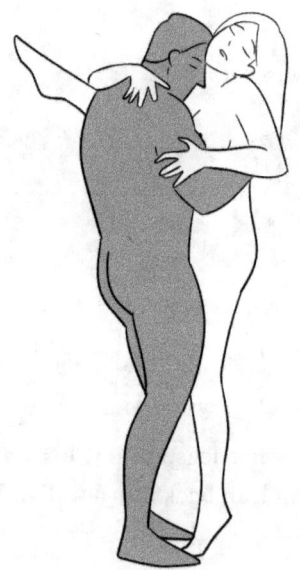

They are both standing, facing each other. She lifts one leg high over his shoulder.

POSITION 112. SUPPORTED CONGRESS

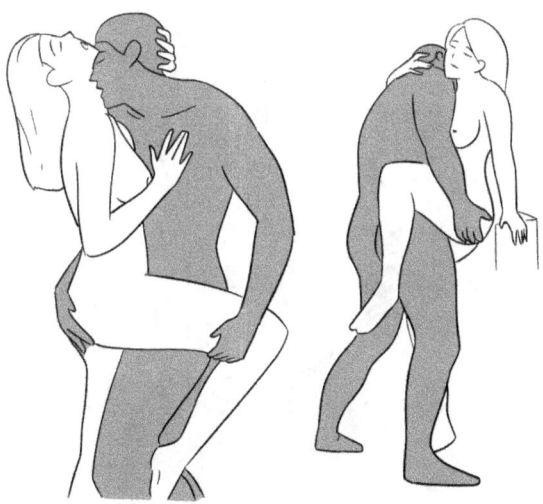

They stand facing each other, with their legs alternating. She lifts one leg and he uses his hand to support it. This position can be free standing or adopted with her backed up against something.

POSITION 113. SUSPENDED CONGRESS

He stands, leaning back against a wall with his legs apart and slightly bent. She sits on him, dangling her legs over his thighs.

POSITION 114. WEEPING WILLOW

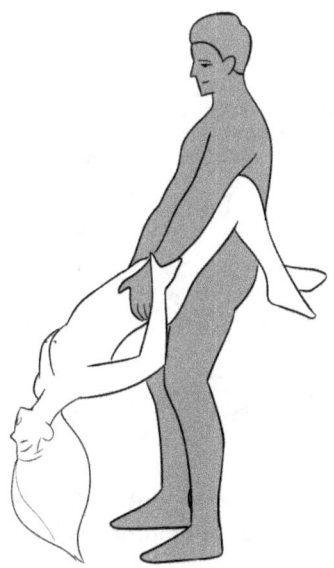

He stands. She wraps her legs around his waist and leans back so her head is near the floor. If he gets tired, he can take a seat.

POSITION 115. WHEELBARROW

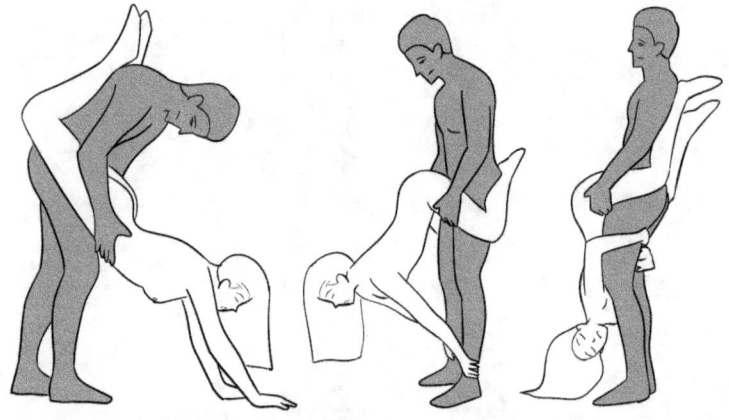

He stands and she stands in front of him, facing away from him. Her hands are on the floor or holding his legs or ankles. Her legs extend past his torso, one leg on each side of him. She can hold onto him with her thighs, wrapping her feet around his waist or on his shoulders.

SIDE ON POSITIONS

Side positions are great for relaxed sex. If you are sleepy or when your body is otherwise not up to other positions, side by side is the answer. It is also highly intimate, and with the often-slow nature of the intercourse, the man can usually last much longer.

POSITION 116. TRANSVERSE LUTE

They are both on their sides, facing each other.

They hold each other close, and he slides up and down her body.

POSITION 117. CICADA TO THE SIDE

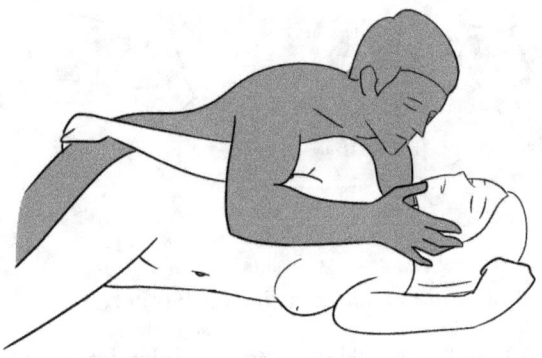

They are both on their sides. She faces away from him. She looks back to him.

POSITION 118. MANDARIN DUCKS

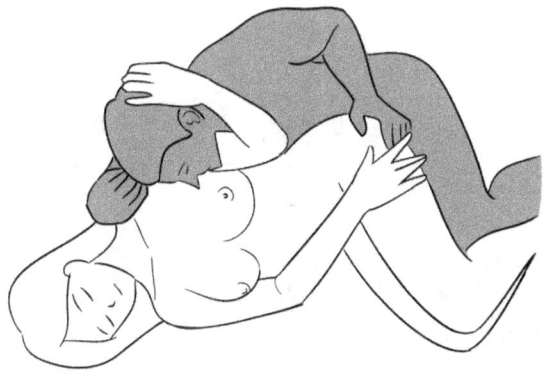

They are both on their sides. She faces away from him. Their legs are bent, and his knees fit behind hers. She can allow for deeper penetration by bringing her knees to her chest.

POSITION 119. TWO FISHES

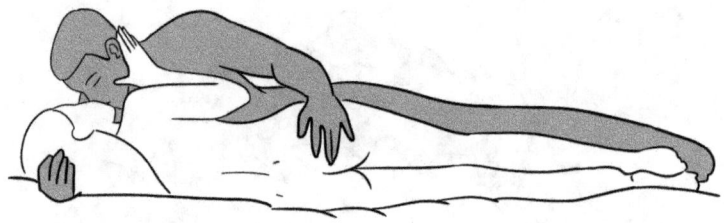

They are both on their sides facing each other, with their legs stretched out.

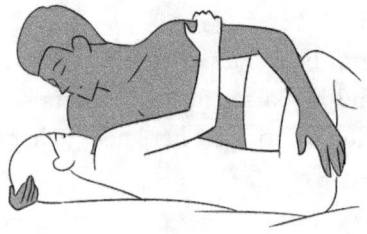

Once he is inside her, she places her legs on top of his.

POSITION 120. 5TH POSTURE

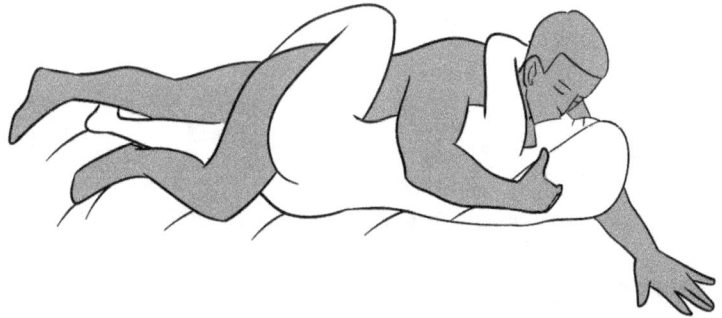

They both lie on their sides, facing each other. His top leg is in between her legs, and they hold each other close. She rests her top leg on his. She can raise her leg higher on his body to allow for deeper penetration.

MISCELLANEOUS POSITIONS

POSITION 121. AUTUMN DOG

She takes a standing position, keeping her legs straight and placing her head and forearms on the floor. He backs up to her, with his feet on either side of hers, until their bums are touching. He keeps his legs fairly straight and touches the floor. He uses his hand to guide his penis inside her, then places it back onto the floor.

POSITION 122. FITTER-IN

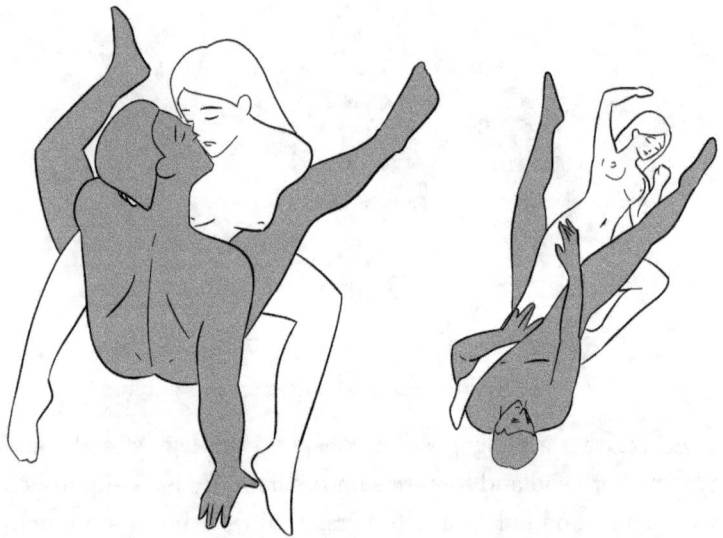

They are both sitting upright, with their groins together. One of her legs is on top of his and the other is underneath his. From here, they can lean back onto their hands or lie back completely.

POSITION 123. DRAWING THE BOW

She lies on her side and raises her top leg high in the air. He lies on her bottom leg so they make a plus sign. He faces her back.

They hold each other's legs with their hands.

POSITION 124. SCISSORS

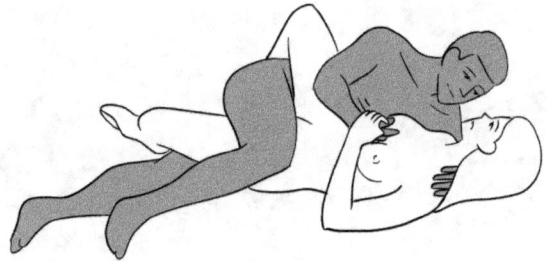

She lies on her side and he lies next to her, facing her back. His bottom leg is under her bottom leg, and his top leg is hooked over her bottom leg. She raises her top leg and turns onto her back to face him, hooking the leg over his waist.

POSITION 125. SITTING ON TOP OF THE WORLD

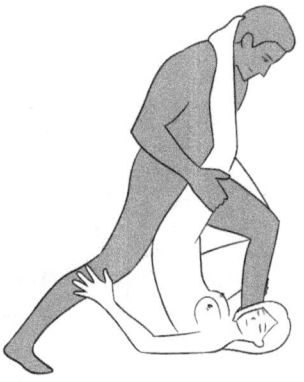

She lies on her back and lifts her legs high in the air, lifting her lower back off the floor. He steps through her legs so one foot is near her head and the other is behind her. One of her legs is angled in between his legs and up his torso, so her foot is near his shoulder.

POSITION 126. SEAGULLS ON THE WING

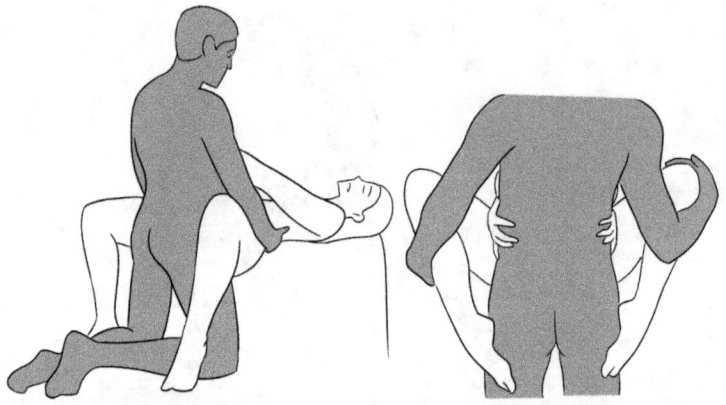

She sits on the edge of a bed (or something similar) with her legs dangling over the edge. She lies back and spreads her legs. He kneels in front of her, between her legs.

She can hook her feet on his buttocks or around his waist.

BONUS - ORAL POSITIONS

These oral position were not part of the original version, so I added them as a bonus instead of retitling the entire book.

ALL FOR HER

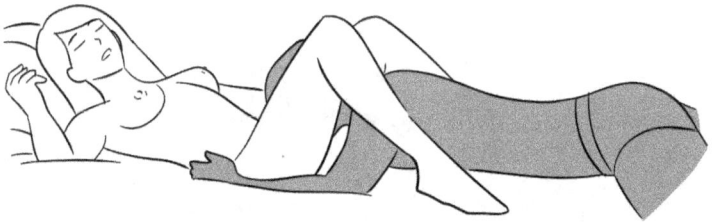

She lies on her back, with her legs spread and feet planted flat. He lies on his stomach, with his head between her legs at her groin.

LEAN BACK

He sits with his legs stretched out in front of him. She kneels astride him, with one knee on either side of his body. She leans back and thrusts her hips up. He bends forward at his torso to meet her groin with his mouth.

RIDING HIS FACE

He lies on his back, with his feet planted on the floor. Facing towards his head, she kneels with one knee on either side of his head and sits on his face.

SIDEWAYS 69

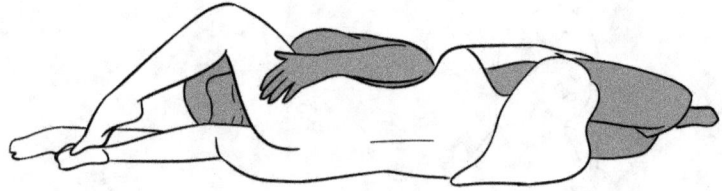

They both lie on their sides, facing each other. They are inverted, so that their mouths are at each other's groins.

69 HER ON TOP

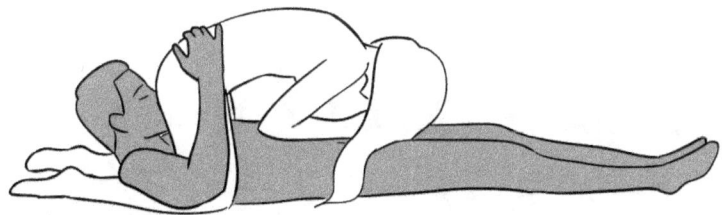

He lies flat on his back. Facing towards his feet, she kneels over him, placing her knees on either side of his upper torso. She bends to meet his groin and he raises his head to meet hers.

69 HIM ON TOP

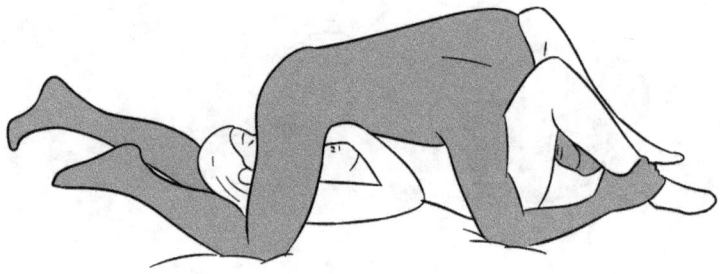

She lies on her back, with her feet on the floor and her legs spread. He faces her feet and kneels, placing his knees on either side of her head. Their heads are in between each other's legs.

STANDING 69

He stands. Her groin is at his mouth, and her legs are wrapped around his head/neck. He helps to hold her up with his hands on her buttocks. Her mouth is on his groin.

THANKS FOR READING

Dear reader,

Thank you for reading *126 Sex Positions Guaranteed To Spice Up Your Bedroom*.

If you enjoyed this book, please leave a review where you bought it. It helps more than most people think.

Don't forget your FREE book chapters!

You will also be among the first to know of FREE review copies, discount offers, bonus content, and more.

Go to:

https://offers.SFNonfictionBooks.com/Free-Chapters

Thanks again for your support.

REFERENCES

Arbuthnot, F. Burton, Richard. (1991). *The Illustrated Kama Sutra : Ananga-Ranga and Perfumed Garden - The Classic Eastern Love Texts.* Park Street Press.

DiCarlo, G. (2014). *Abundant Vitality: Reclaim the Energy of Your Youth Through the Practice of Taoist sexology.* BookBaby.

Jameson, J. Strauss, N. (2012). *How to Make Love Like a Porn Star: A Cautionary Tale.* It Books.

Liu, S. (2011). *Secrets of Dragon Gate: Ancient Taoist Practices for Health, Wealth, and the Art of Sexual Yoga.* TarcherPerigee.

Nerve.com. (2003). *Position of the Day: Sex Every Day in Every Way.* Chronicle Books.

Richardson, D. (2003). *The Heart of Tantric Sex: A Unique Guide to Love and Sexual Fulfillment.* Bedroom Books.

Richardson, D. Richardson, M. (2010). *Tantric Sex for Men: Making Love a Meditation.* Destiny Books.

Riley, D. Riley, K. (2002). *Tantric Secrets for Men: What Every Woman Will Want Her Man to Know about Enhancing Sexual Ecstasy.* Destiny Books.

AUTHOR RECOMMENDATIONS

Teach Yourself Tantric Sex

Start feeling pleasure like you never have before, because this is the biggest sexual awakening you'll ever have.

Get it now.

www.SFNonfictionBooks.com/Learn-Tantric-Sex

Discover How to Use Yoga as Medicine

Add this book to your collection, because with it you can use yoga to heal your mind, body, and spirit.

Get it now.

www.SFNonfictionBooks.com/Curing-Yoga

ABOUT AVENTURAS

Aventuras has three passions: travel, writing, and self-improvement. She is also blessed (or cursed) with an insatiable thirst for general knowledge.

Combining these things, Miss Viaje spends her time exploring the world and learning. She takes what she discovers and shares it through her books.

www.SFNonfictionBooks.com

- amazon.com/author/aventuras
- goodreads.com/AventurasDeViaje
- facebook.com/AuthorAventuras
- instagram.com/AuthorAventuras

www.ingramcontent.com/pod-product-compliance
Lightning Source LLC
Chambersburg PA
CBHW071453080526
44587CB00014B/2098